GHOST STORIES *of* GEORGIA

True Tales of Ghostly Hauntings

Chris Wangler

LONE PINE

Lone Pine Publishing International

The Publisher: Lone Pine Publishing International
Distributed by Lone Pine Publishing
1808 B Street NW, Suite 140
Auburn, WA 98001
USA

Websites: www.lonepinepublishing.com
www.ghostbooks.net

National Library of Canada Cataloguing in Publication Data

Wangler, Chris, 1974-
    Ghost stories of Georgia / Chris Wangler.

    ISBN-13: 978-1-894877-74-9
    ISBN-10: 1-894877-74-8

    1. Ghosts--Georgia. 2. Tales--Georgia. I. Title.

GR110.G4W35 2006   398.2'09758'05   C2006-901520-1

Photo Credits: Every effort has been made to accurately credit photographers. Any errors or omissions should be directed to the publisher for changes in future editions. The photographs in this book are reproduced with the kind permission of the following sources: Corbis (p. 207); Hatem El-Toudy (p. 18); Sheryl Griffin (p.141); Alvaro Heinzen (p. 33); Library of Congress (p. 4–5: HABS GA,58-MOBE,1-7; p. 22: HABS GA,58-MOBE,1-5; p. 38: HABS GA,90-MID,1-7; p. 41: HABS GA,90-MID,1-10; p. 44: HABS, GA,26-SAV.V,2-53; p. 54: HABS GA,123-AUG,8-2; p. 65: DIG-cwpb-03150; p. 68: HABS, GA,26-SAV.V,2-70; p. 71: HABS, GA,26-SAV.V,2-69; p. 73: HABS, GA,26-SAV.V,2-137; p. 77: HABS GA,108-COLM,31-2; p. 80: USZ62-53046; p. 82: HABS GA,11-MACO,17-1; p. 85: HABS GA,11-MACO,17-2; p. 152: HABS GA,26-SAV,24-7; p. 155: HABS, GA,26-SAV,73-1; p. 158: HABS, GA,26-SAV,73-4; p. 165: HABS GA, 26-SAV,21-1; p. 167: HABS GA, 26-SAV,21-3; p. 170: USZ62-5824; p. 228: HABS, GA,26-SAV,15-1; p. 233: HABS, GA,26-SAV,15-4; p. 236: USZ61-2146; p. 239: HABS GA,61-ATLA,14-1); Marietta Museum of History (p. 49).

PC: P5

To Miriam, gone but not forgotten

Contents

Introduction

So why does Georgia have so many great ghost stories? For many reasons, of course, but the rich history and colorful personalities of Savannah are as good a place any to start. Founded by James Edward Oglethorpe in 1733, the city was laid out in a grid with 24 public squares. The South's burgeoning trade in cotton, which would eventually lead to the Civil War, brought great wealth to the city, attracting planters and merchants who built spectacular homes in a variety of styles (Georgian, Gothic Revival, Federal, etc.) and filled them with expensive art and furnishings from Europe. Because Oglethorpe's squares were adjacent to many of these lavish buildings, their owners adorned them with fountains, benches, gardens and memorials to persons of influence.

By the 1950s, however, much of the city's historic heritage was at risk of being lost forever. The creation and maintenance of the Savannah National Historic District, which covers 2.2 square miles and includes more than 1500 restored buildings, has ensured the preservation of a historically rich and unique place. Savannah's ghosts have survived the historical upheavals, shifting fortunes and restoration work, so I have devoted an entire chapter to them. My hope was to reflect some of the magic of the city captured in John Berendt's best-selling book, *Midnight in the Garden of Good and Evil*, a saucy nonfiction story whose flamboyant characters and chilling scenarios have caused some to mistake it for a novel.

Of course, Savannah was not the only key city in the state's history, nor the only one that captures Georgia's unmistakable Southern charms. Islands along Georgia's coast, including St. Simons, are equally rich in ghostly lore, as are the cities of Augusta and Macon. Today, many ghost stories originate in Atlanta, one of the country's fastest growing cities with a population of nearly 4.5 million.

One unexpected center of haunted activity is Milledgeville, which served as the state capital from shortly after the American Revolution until 1868, when it was moved by the Reconstruction government to Atlanta. The survival of some of the city's haunted historic buildings can be attributed in part to General William T. Sherman's mysterious decision to spare the city on his way from Atlanta to Savannah during the War Between the States.

Having vowed to "make Georgia howl," Sherman led 65,000 Federal troops from the Carolinas to Atlanta and on to Savannah on his infamous March to the Sea. By November 1864, he had cut a path of carnage some 80 miles wide, sacked three state capitals and brought an end to the nation's bloodiest conflict. Some of the resistance he encountered from Confederate troops and ordinary citizens along the way is documented in this collection.

Other Civil War stories focus on key fortifications or places—such as the Ezekiel Harris House near Augusta or Marietta's Kennesaw House—which unexpectedly assumed an important role. What gives these stories life, of course, is less the drama of the circumstances and more the heroic soldiers and generals involved.

Georgia has seen its share of celebrities, from famous writers (Margaret Mitchell, Flannery O'Connor) and principled leaders (Jimmy Carter, Martin Luther King) to rollicking entertainers (Ray Charles, Otis Redding) and unforgettable athletes (Ty Cobb). In this collection you will find a handful of celebrities (Joel Chandler Harris, author of the Uncle Remus stories for children, and Girl Scouts founder Juliette Gordon Low), but also wealthy tycoons (Godfrey Barnsley, Leonidas A. Jordan), eccentrics (Methodism founder John Wesley) and even some unbearably wretched human beings (Sam Walker, Marion Stembridge). That their ghost stories are still recited today is indicative not only of their powerful legacies, but also of Georgia's pivotal role in the history of the American South.

Acknowledgments

Nancy Foulds and Carol Woo, shepherds of this wayward beast, deserve gratitude for their endless patience and candor during the writing of this book. I would also like to thank Bernice Johnson of the Macon Public Library and Dr. Fred Samuelson, who offered some excellent advice. The gift of storytelling comes naturally to many Southerners. I am grateful to all those who recounted their stories, especially Georgia Schmit, Chris Jurgensen and Thomas Wilkinson. Others requested that their names not be included in the text. Let me take this opportunity to thank you: you know who you are.

1
Tragic
Love

Mary the Wanderer
St. Simons Island

When Mary McRae arrived in New York, she was utterly alone. She had boarded a ship headed for New York with her parents and older brother hoping for a fresh start in the New World. However, their voyage was struck by tragedy when disease spread quickly on board. Her father was the first to catch smallpox, followed by her brother, Stuart; they died one after another. Her mother was stronger, but she too eventually succumbed, as did almost everyone on board. As the dead piled up, the bodies were cast overboard for fear of the infection spreading to the remaining passengers.

At 13, Mary knew she could find work in a factory as a seamstress, but without any real skills she still felt like a child. Unable to carry her parents' heavy trunk, she sold their possessions as soon as she got off the ship. As she wandered the streets, she saw girls her age begging for alms or dressed in suggestive clothing, sidling up to bucktoothed sailors. She hurried along. Where would she live? What would she eat?

She found refuge in a church for an evening service and a small repast. As she entered the crowded quarters, her embroidered handkerchief, which belonged to her mother, slipped out of her coat pocket onto the dirty floor.

"Here you are, little girl," a Scottish woman said, picking it up and folding it. "Where's your mother, dear?"

The women had a kind face, and looked at Mary with concern. All day, almost in a daze, Mary had hurried around the city, trying to keep busy. Now, suddenly aware of her plight, she began to cry. She was all alone.

The woman comforted her. Amelia Grant and her husband, Jeremy, were from Glasgow, like Mary. They were on their way to Savannah, where Jeremy had found work as a stable hand on a plantation. The Grants took pity on Mary and decided to take care of her until she could stand on her own.

Mary promised not to burden the couple. She only wished to accompany them to Savannah, where she might find work, and then they would part ways. But during the long train journey, she and Amelia became close, playing cards and talking about their impressions of the New World—the large swathes of land, the variety of people and the promise of opportunity. In spite of the age disparity, they were cut from the same Scottish tartan: proud, hardworking, independent.

The Grants set up in a small servant house near the stables. Mary helped Amelia with many of her daily tasks. The grief over her family's deaths overcame Mary on occasion, so she tried to stay busy. Shunning more feminine work, Mary spent as much time as she could in the stables, brushing the horses and helping Jeremy keep them in top condition.

One day, Mr. Raymond Demere, a wealthy planter from St. Simons Island, visited the Marston plantation, and Jeremy was expected to tend to his magnificent horses. As Demere toured the ranch, he was impressed by Mary's hardworking demeanor.

"Mr. Demere asked after you, Mary," Jeremy said over dinner the same night. "I think he has a soft spot in his heart."

"Soft spot, indeed," Amelia said dubiously.

Jeremy continued. "He wants you to come to St. Simons to work as a ward. He says the opportunities are great for a young woman with a good head on her shoulders."

Mary was tempted by the offer. The Marstons had never hired her, having no need of more help, and sometimes she felt more of burden than a help to them. Besides, her grief over the loss of her family was finally subsiding, and she felt a great surge of independence as she reached adulthood.

For her part, Amelia was divided. Mr. Demere seemed almost too nice, too understanding of Mary's plight, but she was aware, too, that Mary's lack of family meant she had no dowry. Mary had now blossomed into a great beauty with fiery red locks and pale skin. Her chances of making a good match would dwindle by the time she reached her 20s— a shame, really, since she would make a fine wife and an excellent mother.

In the end, Mary left the Grants. She was given a small room in the servants' quarters facing the ocean.

The Grove, as Demere's estate was called, was an exquisite cotton plantation, run with an iron hand by Mr. Demere. Mr. Demere's wife, Anne, was no Amelia, but she ran all the domestic tasks on the plantations with remarkable, almost businesslike efficiency.

Mary threw herself into her work, proving herself an apt pupil both in the kitchen and on the grounds. She asked Mr. Demere many questions about running the plantation, and he obliged her with answers. In time, Mary became the most valued hand on the plantation, the equal of any older, more experienced servant.

Now and then Mary missed Amelia, but the sweeping beauty of the island enchanted her, reminding her of the vacations she took with her family on Killarney. She liked to carry a lamp around the island at dusk, exploring the shore and rejoicing in the sounds of the birds overhead. Her favorite path soon formed a narrow trail, from which the best views of the island's scenery could be taken in, and she came to know it so well that she could close her eyes and follow it in the dark, led only by the sounds of the waves crashing against the shore.

By the time Mary turned 18, she had a new preoccupation: Raymond, Jr., the master's younger son. A wild card, prone to running against the crusty grain of plantation mores, Raymond was the opposite of Joseph, his more serious brother, who had recently left to assume control of one of his father's plantations. The brothers stood to inherit their father's sizeable holdings, but Raymond seemed aloof from the cotton business, preferring to ride his mustang, regale a group of slaves with one of his adventure tales or spend hours alone in his skiff, rowing along the shoreline.

Mary had a remarkable effect on Raymond. He became a true gentleman around her—less wild, less brash, less like his father. The two took many strolls around the grounds, and Raymond would tell her about New Orleans and Charleston and his hopes for the future. Mr. Demere, a harsh man, disapproved of his son's rebellious streak and his new interest in Mary, and belittled him whenever he could. Mary was careful to keep her distance from the tension between the two, but she was falling hopelessly in love with Raymond, Jr.

A year or so had passed when one day, Mr. Demere escorted Mary into the stable. Of late he had been looking at her a lot, not disapprovingly, as he did at all the slaves, but with admiration and possibly something more sinister. As they walked into the stable, Mary thought it strange that Robert, the stable hand, was nowhere in sight. Mr. Demere led her to a berth and stopped.

"Mary," he said with forced tenderness, "I want to present this horse to you for all you have done for me and the Grove."

Mary looked over the elaborate wooden stable door. It was Majestic, the finest mare in the stable. Mary had groomed her on many occasions, and grew to adore her shiny, healthy coat and sensitive eyes. She was overwhelmed with joy, but was reluctant to take the gift.

"I can't accept her, Mr. Demere. She's your best mare."

"And you're my best ward, Mary. I expect you and the slaves to take good care of her, but I want her to be yours."

"But I don't ride well," Mary said.

"Tomorrow I will give you a proper riding lesson."

The next day, they set out early. Mr. Demere sat behind Mary in the saddle, allowing her to share his hold on the fine woven reins. As Mary had suspected, his manner with the horses was the same as his manner with the slaves: harsh. With violent motions, he taught her how to stop the horse, how to turn and how to whip. The lesson got longer and longer, and Mary soon noticed that they had come to the other side of the island.

"Let's pick up some speed," Demere said, whipping the mare.

Mary squirmed a bit as he pressed himself against her back and crouched into gallop position. As he pushed the horse harder and harder, Mary became frightened and wanted to get off.

"Stop!" she exclaimed.

"Very well," he said, smiling at her anxiety. "Let us stop for a while."

They had arrived at a giant oak tree in a clearing. Underneath, an exquisite lunch with wine had been laid out. The wind whispered through the trees as the warm sun shone down on them, and Mary became very suspicious.

They ate in silence. Increasingly wary of Demere's intentions, Mary refused the wine and only nibbled on her food.

Planters were known for their indulgences, and regularly took slaves to bed; while wards were different—better treated, perhaps—they were no less prone to the unwanted willful desires of their masters. If the situation became unbearable, as it seemed it would, Mary could leave, but then she'd no longer see Raymond, Jr. The thought scared her because, more than anything else, she feared to be alone again, as she was so long ago.

Demere moved closer to her and gazed deeply into her eyes. "Mary, I want to tell you something," he began. "Sometimes I find myself looking at you…"

Just then, Mary and Mr. Demere heard the sounds of hooves in the distance. It was Raymond, Jr., galloping power- fully toward them. Dust rose up in his wake. When he had reached them, he reared up on his horse and hoisted Mary up into his saddle. They rode away swiftly, almost at the same pace as she had with Demere, but Mary now felt safe and secure. It happened so quickly that all Mr. Demere could do was shake his head. He had been caught red-handed.

Once they were safely away, Raymond slowed his pace. The pair remained silent, unsure of what had just happened. Mary had been spared the indignity of Mr. Demere's advances, but she worried that Raymond was deeply hurt by his father's unfaithfulness.

When they arrived at the stable, unseen, Raymond dis- mounted, then lifted Mary down, spinning her exuberantly in the air. She blushed.

"I want to thank you," she said.

Raymond smiled but looked troubled. "Mary, I must speak with you. I've seen how my father looks at you. It's ter- rible. I want us to leave this plantation, to start anew on the mainland, away from him and his cruelties. Perhaps we'll be poor, but we will have each other."

As they embraced, dark clouds swirled overhead. A storm, promised for days on end, was finally ready to burst. The animals in the barn sensed it, as did Raymond, who said, "Let's get inside. I must decide what to tell my parents."

Mr. Demere was soaked when he returned after them. The heavy rain outside, made more violent by powerful gales, seemed to mirror his foul mood. "Where are they?" Mr. Demere demanded of his wife, barely concealing his rage, though worried that the couple had made report of his advances on Mary.

Just then, Mary and Raymond entered the house, hand in hand. Both seemed older, strengthened by the love they now shared.

"Father, Mother, I'm leaving the Grove. Mary and I are to be married. All I want is the money promised to me, as it was promised and given to Joseph."

"Raymond, don't be ridiculous," Mr. Demere barked. "You are little more than a boy. You have no profession, no talents of any kind. Mary needs a real man, not a boy like you. I refuse to allow you to run away and squander our fortune. You have always made poor decisions, and this is another."

Raymond, Jr., glared at his father. He wanted desperately to tell on him, to reveal the truth at long last, not only about Mary but about all the others, too, but he couldn't hurt his mother. The tension from this secret was almost unbearable, coloring every word of the conversation, but neither party could stand to break it as Mrs. Demere stood by, unaware of what had happened earlier that day and for years before that.

Finally Mrs. Demere spoke up, the voice of reason. "Raymond, please stay and think about your decision—for my sake."

"Listen to your mother, boy. She and I know what you need much better than you ever will. If you try to marry this…this…servant, I won't give you a penny!"

Raymond, red with rage, moved to strike his father, but held back at the last moment. He refused to let anger rule him, as it did his father.

Calmly, he said, "I'll be back later."

Mary tried to follow him. "Take me with you."

"No. Stay here, Mary. I will return for you after I have some time to think. I promise."

Raymond stormed out of the house, as he did when he needed time to himself, headed in the direction of his little boat. In his haste he failed to notice how powerfully the wind blew.

As Mary hurried to her quarters, Mr. Demere caught up with her, pulled her into a pantry and tried to kiss her. Mary broke free from his embrace and ran off. As she did, he warned her, "If you tell Mrs. Demere about us, I'll kill you, you Scottish witch."

Mary retrieved her trusty old lamp in her room and lit it. Then she found her warmest shawl and prepared to venture out into the storm. With darkness descending, she worried more and more about Raymond. She was better aware of the risks of venturing out with a hurricane brewing, so she was confident that she could find him and bring him home.

She set out. But even with a scarf tightly wrapped around her head, the wind was too brisk, making a mess of her hair. The rain, falling in large buckets, lashed her face and made it

Mary retrieved her trusty old lamp and prepared to venture out into the storm.

nearly impossible to find her way. Fortunately she knew the area better than anyone.

After searching and shouting at length, she came to the small dock where Raymond tied his boat. He was nowhere to be seen, and she feared the worst as she looked out on the seas churning angrily, with giant waves crashing on the shore. She thought of her family so long ago, their diseased bodies disappearing beneath the waves of the mighty Atlantic.

Suddenly she spotted something in the distance. She ran as fast as she could against the gale-force winds, nearly falling over and tripping as she reached the water. It was an oar from Raymond's boat—or rather, part of an oar. It had been shattered in half, and Mary began to cry as she imagined the worst: that Raymond had been caught at sea and pulled under. His body was missing, as was the rest of his boat.

No one knows what happened next. It's possible that Mary lost her will to live then, and threw herself over the bluff and drowned. It's equally probable that the hurricane conditions proved too overpowering, dragging her into the choppy waters. Whatever the case, no one saw Mary and Raymond ever again. In spite of much searching by the Demeres and the local authorities, their bodies were never recovered.

But their spirits, it is said, remain on St. Simons, united in death. A light, thought to be Mary's lantern, can be seen near the south shore of the island whenever a violent storm comes on. Only those who can endure the brutal weather see it, and they are often struck by the experience, since it seems as if a cloaked figure is searching through the darkness for something or someone. One can only assume it is Mary the Wanderer in search of her lost lover.

The Green Lady

BERRY COLLEGE

Situated on some 28,000 acres, 65 miles northwest of Atlanta, Berry College is one of Georgia's most respected postsecondary institutions, with an open, interdenominational mandate. Academics are the focus, but the scenic forests, lakes and mountains nearby add greatly to its appeal. More than 100 years after its founding, many of the college's students still spend time exploring these natural areas, and some have crossed paths with some eerie ghosts.

Today, Stretch Road connects the mountain campus to the main campus. Back in the 1940s, long before the mountain campus had been built, young lovers would take the road into the remote woods in search of privacy. One of the most frequently told stories at the college, of the so-called Green Lady, originates along this dark, shaded road.

Lamar and Becky (pseudonyms, for their names are now forgotten) were both students at the college. Becky was raised in a strict Baptist home, while Lamar was staunchly Catholic; both feared parental disapproval, but they were irresistibly, even magnetically, drawn to one another.

One spring evening, the couple set out on Stretch Road, as they had many times before. Some versions of the story suggest that the couple was in a car that fateful night, but they actually rode their bicycles.

Upon arriving in an intimate clearing, Lamar and Becky settled down for a picnic. Beer lightened the mood, and as the sun set they began to kiss. Half an hour later, they lay peacefully in each other's arms without a care in the world.

When the conversation turned to their future plans, they began to quarrel. At first it was only a lighthearted discussion about their relationship—the kind that couples arrive at following the passionate initial stages of courtship. Becky soon began to cry, and she stubbornly jumped on her bike and headed down the steep slope back to the campus.

Wrenched back to earth by their first fight, Lamar consumed the remaining bottles of beer to take his mind off the situation. However, he couldn't stop worrying about Becky on her bicycle on Stretch Road late at night, alone. The sky was now black and overcast. How could he let her take off as she did? He loved her and he wanted to apologize, so he set off in pursuit.

It never occurred to Lamar that Becky had turned around and was riding back in his direction. Although we'll never know exactly what caused her to return, it's reasonable to assume that she wanted to make up with Lamar. Unfortunately, their mutually good intentions could not prevent a tragedy.

A light rain had become a downpour, and visibility became limited on the typically foggy mountain pass. Lamar entered a sharp turn, flying on his bicycle at nearly 30 miles per hour. With his judgment clouded by alcohol, he failed to notice Becky laboriously pedaling up the road with her head down. He ran into her at full speed, running her over. Becky's bike was made of heavy steel and she was not wearing a helmet, so the fall was serious. Her head was starting to bleed heavily.

Lamar's desperate attempts to revive her failed; she was drifting out of consciousness. He waited for a few minutes, hoping to spot a passing car, but none came, so he covered

Over the years, many eyewitnesses have spotted a ghost on Stretch Road.

Becky with his jacket and raced to the campus. By the time an ambulance arrived nearly 45 minutes later, Becky had lost too much blood. She lay dead on the road, soaking wet from the rain.

Lamar was inconsolable. He felt responsible and considered killing himself, but his faith pulled him through. Though he went on to live a long life, he never loved another woman and was only able to talk about the incident shortly before his own death.

Over the years, many eyewitnesses have spotted a ghost on Stretch Road. One story involves a sophomore who was driving back to the campus on a rainy night in August. It was unusually foggy that night, so much so that she was driving well under the speed limit and using her high beams to illuminate the lonely road ahead.

Not far from where Becky was killed, the girl noticed something eerie on the side of the road. At first she thought it was a trick of perception caused by the car lights and awkward driving conditions. A brilliant, unnatural shade of green light, glowing in the distance, convinced her otherwise.

She stopped the car and got out to get a better look. The light was coming from about 50 yards into trees, so it was hard to make out through all the branches. The girl began to walk toward it, perceiving it as the figure of a person. "Hello?" she asked, wondering who would be out walking on such a terrible night. "Do you need help?" No answer.

For a second, the light seemed to disappear behind a tree trunk. Noticing that the figure seemed unaware of her presence, the girl moved forward, cocking her head to the right and then to the left to see if she could spot it again. But the figure had vanished.

She was beginning to get soaked, so the girl turned back to her car. Just before she opened the door to get in, she noticed something out of the corner of her eye. It was the figure, only now it was 10 feet away from the trunk and glowing like a lightning bug! The milky-white apparition wore an old-fashioned green dress and a bonnet. But her most conspicuous feature was her icy cold gaze. As the girl squinted to get a better look, she realized that the apparition's eyes were missing! She screamed, then jumped in her car and sped away, never to return. She had just seen the Green Lady.

Other sightings ended similarly. While the Green Lady appears to mean no harm, each eyewitness walks away with horrible feelings of loss and dread. As to why her eyes are missing, we can only speculate. Perhaps because her eyes failed to save her on the night she was killed, she cannot see in the afterlife. Whatever the case, nothing can interrupt her endless search for Lamar and the love they once knew.

The Public House
ROSWELL

In Georgia before the Civil War, many towns were mill towns, producing cotton material, yarn and thread. It was not at all uncommon for such mills to sell their own goods (and other supplies) to their workers and to the public. In Roswell, a kind of company town, the store run by the Roswell Manufacturing Company enjoyed a monopoly on almost all domestic and industrial goods. If locals needed something, whether it was cornmeal, undergarments or washing boards, chances were that the mill store was the only place to buy it.

The mill offered credit to its workers and paid them in scrip that could be used in the mill store. Many workers overextended their credit, fell into debt and were forced to work overtime for measly wages or to pay their debts in other ways. Perhaps worst of all, the prices in the store were artificially inflated because there was no competition. For the workers—and for the locals—it was a "lose, lose" situation. With no hope, many turned to whiskey to drown their sorrows. But it, too, like everything else, was sold (and sometimes even distilled) by the mill owners.

This situation, unfair in peacetime, was greatly aggravated by the Civil War. The Confederate Army, with a seemingly inexhaustible need for uniforms, supplies and food, often left the mill stores empty. People would wait for hours in line, expecting to buy a small amount of thread or firewood, only to be turned away when supplies ran out. Tempers flared and arguments broke out.

Such was the situation in Roswell in April 1864. With a Confederate defeat at hand, the Southern currency had become worthless. Only Yankee dollars had any value, and most of this money was in the hands of the mill owners and the occupying Union soldiers. The locals were forced to conceal their livestock and produce from the Federals, who could confiscate it without warning and then barter it for overpriced staples at the company store. The store would then trade for goods at a pittance, then sell them at a substantial profit.

Katherine was a young woman whose father had fallen badly into debt, forcing her into servitude at the company store. Her friends and fellow citizens stood waiting in line when the store opened early in the morning, and everyone wanted a handout or a favor. Many would bring beeswax or tallow, but often the amounts were insufficient to barter for what they needed. Katherine's boss, Mr. Johnstone, firmly on the side of the mill owners, instructed her to show no sympathy. "Business as usual," he would say arrogantly. "I don't care what happens outside the store. We have rules here, and they will be obeyed."

Her life seemed hopeless. Her father was infirm from too many years in the mill, and deeply in debt. Only her new beau, a Union soldier named Michael she had met only a week before, gave her hope for the future, but even their love was a long shot in such troubled times. Still, it didn't prevent her from thinking about him and their next tryst as the customers approached the counter, each begging for this or asking for an exception with that. It was only a matter of time before something bad happened, before someone snapped under the pressure.

One day, Michael entered the store and approached the counter, decked out in a crisp new blue uniform. As his boots echoed on the wooden floors, the citizens made way, worried that the soldier might confiscate what little they carried in their arms.

"I need a spool of thread to mend our uniforms."

It was an outrageous demand, and everyone knew it. The most anyone could expect was five, maybe six inches of thread. Here was a demand for an entire spool, and for the enemy's war effort no less. But when the soldier produced a single crisp Yankee dollar, Mr. Johnstone responded immediately.

"Of course. Katherine, fetch it immediately!"

"And let me alert you kind citizens," Michael explained, "that there will be no lawlessness in this store as long as the Union flag flies over Roswell Square. I will leave a sentry here to ensure that everything is in order. Good day to you all."

The soldier made his way to the door.

Right before he left, he turned around and said to Mr. Johnstone, "Sir! This thread feels too thick for our mending needle. Please come to my wagon and show my men how to thread it."

Mr. Johnstone nodded at Katherine. "Well, what are you waiting for? Do it."

Katherine rushed outside. Michael hoisted her into his dark wagon. This forbidden meeting, like all the others, was desperate and fleeting, but no less passionate. But he had bad news: the Union suspected the mill was providing material for the Confederate side, so officers had been ordered to take over the mill and arrest some of the men. Katherine, understandably worried about her father and friends, was terribly upset. Michael tried to reassure her by saying that as soon as the Confederates surrendered, they could go north to safety.

Just then, Mr. Johnstone came out to check on Katherine.

"Katherine!" he shouted. "Come in at once!"

"There's no time," Michael said. "Will you marry me?"

Katherine was speechless.

"Think about it and meet me near the covered bridge at sundown. I love you."

No one knows what happened to the couple. Some say they were killed in a battle near the end of the war, others say they eventually made it north as planned. Whatever the case, they disappeared from Roswell that night, and were never seen or heard from again—at least not their living selves.

Today, the old mill is a gourmet restaurant called the Public House. Over the years, servers and management have reported a number of unexplained occurrences in the piano bar of the Public House, which served as a loft in the old store where the two young lovers met in secret on several occasions.

One woman from Atlanta, Georgia Schmit, encountered the couple when visiting her sister in Roswell. After a delicious meal at the Public House, they adjourned to the piano bar for some cognac. It was a quiet Tuesday evening, so they found themselves alone in the pleasant but dark room.

As they sipped their drinks, the sisters heard two sets of feet lightly walking across the floor on the other side of the room. The footsteps were quite close together, and one set of them sounded heavier, like a man's. At first the sisters assumed two staff members were cleaning up. But as they listened more carefully in the darkened room, where their sense of hearing seemed more acute, they also heard distinct whispers, as if the two were trying to hide their presence. "Hello," Georgia said, prodding the two strangers to reveal themselves. The sounds stopped immediately. Georgia walked over to their source but saw nothing. There was no exit nearby, and no trace that anyone had been there.

Assuming that two of the staff members were involved in something illicit, the sisters returned to the restaurant and asked the hostess about the activity in piano bar. She smiled, then related the story about the two ghostly lovers who were seen or heard on occasion. Georgia and her sister were dumbfounded. Neither believed in ghosts. "Well, how do you know it was them?" she asked. "Couldn't it have been two of the staff members?"

"No, I'm afraid not. There's only one entrance to the room, and it's the one you came through. If there were people already in the room, you would have seen them leave. If they entered after you, they would have passed you."

From that day forward, both Georgia and her sister believed in ghosts.

Staff members have also reported mischievous tricks played by the secretive spirits, and visitors have seen the apparition of a teenage girl dressed in an old-fashioned blue skirt. Sometimes the ghosts have been known to dance late at night and sit in the chairs that overlook Roswell Square. Although their earthly lives remain a mystery, they appear to have found some security as the resident specters of the Public House.

Emma's Light
St. Simons Island

This story is about fear of the dark—not only the absence of light, but the darkness of death, of loneliness and of the emptiness that accompanies the passing of a loved one. It is, to quote the Gospel of John, a story about "the light which shineth in darkness and the darkness comprehendeth it not."

In a quiet corner of St. Simons Island called Fredericka, there is a very old and simple graveyard called Christ Church. There, among the sea salt encrusted stones, a flickering, otherworldly light shines in the darkness as a reminder of a little girl's fear of the dark.

Emma's fear grew out of childhood. Victoria, her leathery old nurse, would enter her room at night, extinguish the lantern and tell scary stories that she knew by heart. Some of these stories were perversions of famous fairy tales, altered to be much scarier than their antecedents, while others were inventions of Victoria's own twisted mind, reflecting her own childhood fears and twisted obsessions. The stories all revolved around the power of darkness. Being recited in the dark made them even more terrifying to the shy four-year-old.

One of the stories was about little girls who were turned into evil dolls by a witch who lived in a dark cave. In another, a man who lived alone in the woods disguised himself as a friendly old baker. He would come to town, saying he had baked too many gingerbread houses, luring away children who were hungry because they hadn't eaten their dinner. When the children arrived at his house, the imposter would imprison them in his dark basement, starve them and then have his monkey servants bury them alive in a grave behind the house. A character in another story, the Shadow, was also a force of pure evil, obsessed with hunting down little girls who didn't do their chores. Everything he touched died instantly.

Victoria's intention was to get Emma to behave, but the effect was much deeper. The little girl became so terrified of the dark that she began to scream during the night.

For many months this went on. Although Victoria was fired for scaring the little girl, Emma never lost her fear of the dark.

Emma's parents tried everything to help her overcome her fear. Nothing worked. As soon as the sun set and darkness crept into the house, Emma's fears multiplied. When her lamp went out and the darkness descended on her room, her horrid cries pierced the night air. Her father, an otherwise understanding man, grew increasingly impatient. One night, he instructed Emma's new nurse to lock her in her bedroom with no light of any kind. By confronting her fear, he reasoned, his daughter could finally beat it for good. The nurse hesitated at first, but performed the uncomfortable duty nonetheless.

That night, Emma's bloodcurdling screams could be heard nearly a mile away. Soon everyone was out of bed, gathered nervously in the corridor outside her room. Emma's mother begged her husband to unlock the door and light the lamp. Realizing that his daughter was truly, deeply afraid of the dark, he relented, throwing open the door, lighting a candle and apologizing profusely to the quivering girl. Emma's father decided then and there to leave a candle burning in her room every night.

The next day he instructed the nurse to buy as many candles as she could find on the island. Over time, Emma
became obsessive about her candles. She collected candle
stubs wherever she found them, and gradually learned how
to melt them down and use the wax in new candles. She
insisted on a certain kind of beeswax candle, which burned
longer than the tallow varieties and cast a brighter light.
A cedar box was specially constructed for them, and she
took a handful along whenever she went to visit friends.

Her one limitation aside, Emma became a normal, well-
adjusted young woman with many friends. She was a volun-
teer at her church and a Sunday school teacher. As she
matured, she turned her attention to romance. The young
man who caught her fancy, Philip, had recently arrived from
South Carolina to work as a clerk at a shipping firm. He was
tall, intelligent and gregarious.

Their courtship was like a fairy tale. Philip was an accom-
plished pianist, and on his initial visits he performed serious
pieces by Brahms and Mozart to entertain the family. But as
his feelings for Emma deepened, he began to play romantic
favorites—fanciful sonatas by Chopin, Beethoven and Lizst.
He would look at Emma with a piercing glance at the
crescendo of each selection.

Soon they were seeing each other alone. At first Philip
thought nothing of Emma's preference for daytime meetings.
Whenever he asked her for a night-time stroll, she created an
excuse. He began to wonder about it one September evening
when an intense discussion caused them to lose track of
time. They sat alone at the edge of a shimmering pond, holding hands, and before either knew it, the autumn sun had
dipped under the brilliant pink horizon.

Emma never lost her fear of the dark.

"We must get back," Emma said, snapping out of her lover's reverie. Her visceral fear of the dark was taking hold, and she had a desire to tell her beloved about her phobia. But she felt too embarrassed, too ashamed. Her fear, after all, was childish, almost inappropriate. Philip looked at her questioningly, awaiting an explanation. Everything seemed perfect. He suspected something was wrong, but didn't ask as he led her home.

The couple was soon engaged. The families on both sides got along extremely well, and looked forward to the wedding. Emma's family, however, knew of her fear of the dark while Philip and his family had no clue.

The night before the wedding, Philip came to the house to discuss the final preparations. Everything seemed in order, from the flowers to the guests to the elaborate reception, except for one rather significant matter: Emma's fear of the dark. She had managed to keep it from her fiancé for nearly a year. For weeks leading up the wedding she had tried and tried to sleep without her candles lit, tossing and turning and reliving her childhood nightmares. Nothing worked. Now, with her wedding night at hand, she would have to tell Philip.

Emma walked to the window and looked out into the garden.

Philip approached her and grasped her shoulders from behind. "What's wrong?" he asked.

Emma broke down and confessed: "Oh Philip, I...I...am...terrified of the dark."

"That's it?" he exclaimed. "How silly! You needn't worry about that, my dear—or anything else. As your husband, I will love you, as you are, for all time."

Emma was overjoyed. The couple was married the next day at Christ Church in Fredericka. They lived for a year or so in Brunswick, then moved back to St. Simons, where Philip helped his father-in-law manage his growing plantation and related businesses.

At first Philip struggled to cope with the light from Emma's candles. He trained himself to not notice the light whenever it awoke him, but rather to cast his glance on his wife as she slept. The look of tranquility on her face would soon lull him back to sleep.

Emma's candles were ideally suited to her life. Some were longer than others to last through long winter nights, while still others had different wicks, depending on the breezes that might enter her bedroom. When they were ready for storage, Emma tied the candles in neat bundles, labeled them by month and stored them in an impressive wall of cedar trunks in the cellar. Not that she needed so many: even if Emma had five candles burning every night, her supply could have lasted months, even years.

Having accepted Emma's obsession with candle-making, Philip began to buy her the appropriate supplies so she could indulge the security it brought. It took up some of her time, but not so much that he ever seriously worried. The understanding the couple shared cemented their love even more.

But Emma's obsession ultimately took a tragic turn.

One day, while lifting a heavy cauldron of boiling wax, Emma spilled some on her arm. The burns were very severe and soon became infected. After home remedies failed, doctors were summoned to the house and announced that she had come down with yellow fever as well. Emma's condition became steadily worse, and soon she was beyond help.

On her last night, the family doctor emerged from Emma's lit room. "Summon the minister," he instructed the Philip. "Only heaven can help her now."

Philip was heartbroken. With tears welling up, he entered their bedroom. Emma sensed her husband nearby and, in a soft whisper, began to speak.

"Philip, my love," she began, struggling to stay lucid. "I have only one final wish. Whatever happens, please keep a candle burning through the night and after I am dead. I don't want to lie in a dark cemetery alone."

"Of course, Emma. The light will burn always, like my love for you."

Then Emma was gone. She was buried in the Christ Church Cemetery the next day.

Thereafter, every night at dusk without fail, Philip rode in a carriage to her gravestone, lit one of her beeswax candles and placed it in a sturdy lantern. Then he said a prayer for her soul and for his own, that they would be reunited in death. Nothing stopped him in this ritual. Not foul weather, sickness, time or apathy. Philip never remarried and until he himself lay in a grave next to his wife's, he made sure Emma's light shone in the darkness.

Today, the light still shines in the cemetery on St. Simons Island. No one on St. Simons will disclose the location of Emma's gravestone, and the flickering light goes out when it is approached. But it shines all the same, a symbol of one woman's fear, her husband's promise and the love they now share in the world beyond.

Midway Cemetery
MIDWAY

Midway was established in 1752 by Puritan settlers from Connecticut and South Carolina. As their rice, cotton and indigo plantations thrived, the community quickly added to its original 44 citizens. Many of the new additions were slaves who accompanied the settlers. When Midway was fully settled, there were about six slaves for every Puritan, and much of the economic viability of the area was owed to slave labor.

As time passed, more and more of Midway's citizens spent their summers near the coast town of Sudbury, in part to escape diseases such as malaria and yellow fever that were carried by mosquitoes near the inland plantations. The community, like so many others in Georgia, was leveled by Sherman's march. In 1864 Federal troops overran Midway, occupying the buildings and freeing the slaves. By this point the war had become extremely bitter, so Union forces felt no qualms about desecrating the Midway Congregational Church, which, oddly enough, was a symbol of New England Puritanism in the South.

Following the war, the locals were suddenly at a loss; they could not run their plantations without their slaves, nor could they afford to pay for help. A hopeless economic downturn followed, typical of much of South Georgia. The area never truly recovered, although its role in the Revolutionary period lives on in a number of ways. Unbeknownst to many, Midway County was where the flag of independence first flew in the state of Georgia.

The Midway Congregational Church was a symbol of New England Puritanism in the South.

Several patriots are buried in the old Midway Cemetery; founded in 1754, it is one of the most historic in the state.

James Screven, a great Revolutionary War hero and radical, is one of the most famous persons interred there. In 1778, as the English advanced into Georgia to crush the nascent revolutionaries, Screven arrived with 21 militias to aid the locals who had formed a line outside Midway Congregational

Church. He heroically defended the town until he ran into enemy troops and was captured, dying several days later as a wounded prisoner of war. To this day, a nearby county bears his name.

John Stewart, the namesake of nearby Fort Stewart, was another hero who attained the rank of brigadier during the Revolutionary War and served in the subsequent Indian Wars. His great-grandson was Theodore Roosevelt. Other names among the 1,200 graves include the physician Nathan Brownson, who was elected governor after the fall of Augusta in January 1781, and John Elliott, another politician, who served as state senator from 1819 to 1825.

But the past is not resting in peace at the old Midway Cemetery. Even today, the ghosts of two young star-crossed lovers appear in the cemetery, still mourning their futile love more than 150 years after their tragic deaths.

The relationship was doomed from the start. Sylvia Brown, a gorgeous 17-year-old with blond hair, was the daughter of a rich and strict planter. Anthony, whom she fell hopelessly in love with, was a black slave. They met in the stable where Anthony handled the plantation horses Sylvia loved to ride, and they had many opportunities to talk.

A deep bond developed. But because their love was strictly forbidden, Anthony and Sylvia chose to meet in Midway Cemetery. Four nights a week, rain or shine, they would embrace in the shadows in the wee hours. The affair carried on for months.

Meanwhile, Sylvia's parents invited a number of suitors to the house to court her. With a few exceptions, Sylvia detested every single man she met, mostly because they were after her father's money, not her love.

For a long time she never told anyone about Anthony or their late-night trysts. Eventually, driven crazy by her secret passion, she broke down and told her parents she had fallen in love with a stranger. Mr. and Mrs. Brown demanded to know his name. Sylvia clammed up. Her father's anger was notorious, and back then black men could be hanged for even *looking* at white women.

Anthony, too, became increasingly impatient. He was aware that his life could be at risk, but also knew that it meant nothing without Sylvia. One day he had had enough. In a fit of passion he walked up to the Browns' sprawling plantation house and knocked at the front door. He felt that he had to tell Sylvia's family, or he would die.

A black maid answered the door, surprised. Black people were not permitted to call at the houses of white people, and they were especially forbidden to enter through the front door. When Sylvia's parents came to the door, Mr. Brown held a fireplace poker in his hand. "What is your business here, boy?"

By now, Sylvia had joined the group gathered at the door. She burned with embarrassment as she saw Anthony turned away so cruelly. Mustering all her courage, she stepped past her parents and grabbed her love by the arm as he turned to go. "Mother, Father," she said, spinning him around. "This is Anthony. He and I are in love."

Sylvia's parents were shocked and outraged by her announcement. Her father and another man, whose job was to keep the slaves in line, beat Anthony savagely and dragged him away. Sylvia, distraught, was locked in her room and forbidden to come out.

The past is not resting in peace at the Midway Cemetery.

Her parents, hoping to force their daughter to forget about Anthony by forcing her into a respectable marriage, wasted no time in selecting a suitor with Old World money, whose position would be considerably improved with the addition of Sylvia's dowry. Sylvia knew and despised him.

Her anger against her parents grew increasingly bitter. She asked again and again after Anthony, but her father refused to speak to her. On the night before her wedding, she jimmied open her second-story window, crawled out and jumped to the ground, spraining her ankle in the process. She limped through the bushes to the cemetery and climbed over the stone wall. Moonlight illuminated the gravestones and all was quiet. Then Sylvia heard a rope moving heavily against a branch and saw Anthony's naked, bruised body beyond the cemetery wall, hanging from a tree.

She rushed over and desperately tried to bring his body down to the ground, but couldn't release him from the heavy rope. Then she remembered that she still had the knife she had used to open the lock on her window. She scaled the tree and cut him down.

Sylvia moaned in agony, holding him in her arms. Seeing no purpose in life, she took the knife and slit her throat, falling on Anthony's chest. She quickly bled to death. As if to confirm the universal disapproval of their love, the couple was denied burial in the cemetery and was interred instead by the tree where they both perished.

Even to this day, cemetery visitors see two shadowy forms beneath an aged oak tree outside the cemetery. Deeply melancholic, they look hopelessly to a spot in the cemetery where they met in secret so long ago.

Anthony and Sylvia are not the only unusual phenomena at the old Midway Cemetery. Another well-known story involves a bizarre crack in a wall.

The brick wall around the cemetery was built by slaves in 1813. During the construction of the northern portion, two slaves got into a bitter dispute. It festered during the long day, preventing them from finishing the work assigned. When their master saw how little had been done by day's end, he became upset and told them to stay late until the job was done. The slaves mortared more bricks, jawing back and forth as the light failed. Under pressure to finish the job, a conflict ensued, and one of the men bashed the other on the head with a brick. The man fell to the ground, bleeding heavily. He was dead within minutes. When his murderer realized what he had done, he frantically tore up the wall and buried the man underneath. He spent the next few hours racing to rebuild the wall before his master returned early the following morning.

"What happened to your partner?" came the inevitable query.

"He ran away," the slave explained.

Although the dead slave was never mentioned again, the wall that covered him began to crumble at an unusually fast rate. All attempts to patch or repair it were fruitless. Eventually slaves were ordered to tear down that section of the wall and rebuild it. When they did, they uncovered the bones of the murdered slave. Convinced that the cause of the crack in the wall had been discovered, everyone breathed a sigh of relief, and the slaves set out to rebuild the wall. But the crack in the wall returned as soon as they had finished, and it remains there to this day. No satisfactory explanation for the crack has ever been provided.

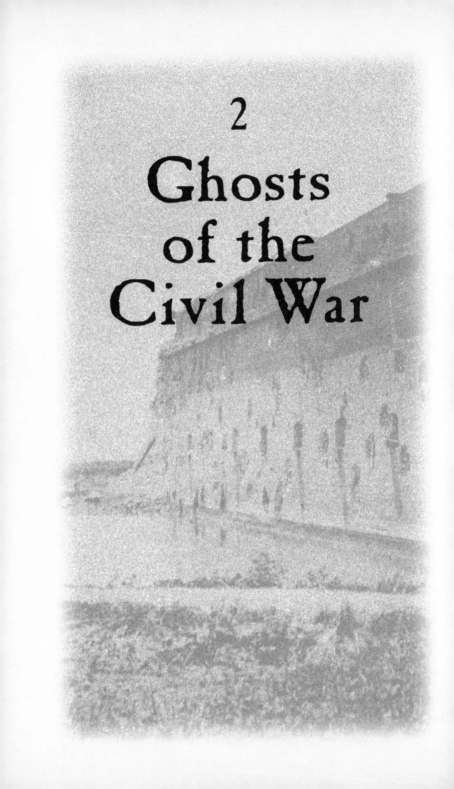

2
Ghosts
of the
Civil War

Kennesaw House

MARIETTA

Just northwest of Atlanta is Marietta. Near the end of the Civil War, much of the industrial town was destroyed because it was along General Sherman's destructive march to Atlanta. One of the historic buildings that survived, Kennesaw House, today positioned on the edge of Kennesaw Mountain National Battlefield Park, is the city's most haunted building. Although claims that 700 ghosts inhabit the former inn are greatly exaggerated, its fascinating history and surprising ghosts make it a key destination for anyone traveling across scenic northwest Georgia.

The red brick building was built in 1845 by Mayor John Glover to serve as a cotton warehouse. In 1855 Dix Fletcher bought the property and converted it into an inn, the Fletcher House Hotel. It was one of the finest establishments in all of Georgia. The building stood right across the street from the Western and Atlantic Railroad depot, so much of its history is intertwined with the movement of goods and people—and, as we shall see, even a fascinating wartime plot by scheming Unionist saboteurs.

During the Civil War, Marietta was an important transportation hub for supplies headed to battlefields in Tennessee and Virginia. The inn's proximity to the railroad and to the Georgia Military Academy made it popular with Union spies who sought to cripple the all-important Confederate supply lines. The innkeeper Fletcher was no spy, but he was a Union sympathizer. So was his son-in-law

Henry Greene Cole, who operated the Marietta Hotel across the street.

A group of 22 Union spies, led by James Andrews, stayed on the second floor of Fletcher's inn on April 11, 1862, the same day that Union General Ormsby Mitchel captured Huntsville, which lay to the north. The unenlisted Andrews, who had traveled across Georgia with his men in civilian clothes, had earned the trust of the Confederates by smuggling quinine, a popular medicine, across battle lines.

The group planned to steal "the General," a Western and Atlantic Railroad engine, after it departed for Chattanooga the next day. En route, they would blow up bridges, tunnels and stretches of track. With the railroad in shambles and a Dixie engine under his command, the Union General Mitchel figured that his forces could easily move from Huntsville to capture Chattanooga.

The hijacking didn't go exactly as planned.

"The General" departed from Atlanta at 4 AM. When the train stopped for breakfast in Big Shanty, as Marietta was then called, the passengers and crew disembarked. Andrews and his men, several of whom were trained railroad engineers, sneaked onto the train, took the controls and set off north for Chattanooga. Big Shanty had no telegraph, so even if the Confederates caught wind of the plot, they would be unable to send word to the next station.

Unfortunately for the raiders, they were spotted boarding the train. The train's conductor, William A. Fuller, set out in pursuit of the steel engine on foot, accompanied by Engineers Jeff Cain and Anthony Murphy. Thus began what became known as the Great Locomotive Chase. After running nearly two miles, the three men found an abandoned platform handcar at Moon's Station. They propelled it, with the help of additional volunteers, down the gentle slope to the Etowah River. There, they boarded "the Yonah," a switch engine, and continued the pursuit.

When the pursuers arrived at the complicated Kingston station, they were forced to abandon "the Yonah" to avoid southbound rail traffic. On foot again, they bypassed the station, commandeered the "the William R. Smith" farther up and set off toward Adairsville. When they came upon torn-up track along the way, they were forced to follow on foot again. North of Adairsville, Fuller and his men boarded "the Texas," a southbound train.

The chase was finally on, but Fuller and his men still had no idea who the mysterious raiders were. At first they assumed they were Union soldiers trying to escape, but they changed their minds when they noticed the damaged rails and cut telegraph wires along the railroad. Clearly a Union plot was underway.

Andrews' raiders, meanwhile, had no idea they were being pursued. Four of them remained in the engine as the 18 others spread themselves through the train, doing whatever they could to sabotage the route behind them. They had mixed success, snipping some telegraph lines but failing in their attempts to destroy the bridges over the Etowah River and Chickamauga Creek. As the conspirators passed stations along the way, puzzled railroad staff and passengers asked about the unusual crew aboard Engineer Fuller's train. Andrews shouted out that he was delivering gunpowder to a Confederate general in Corinth, an excuse that seemed to make sense in a time of war.

Then Andrews spotted "the Texas" in full pursuit. He had to act fast. Two of his men tried to raise a rail to prevent the engine from following them. They failed. Then they tried to jettison rail ties on the tracks, again with no success. Next, they unlatched two boxcars, hoping that they would impede their pursuers. But Fuller and his men were experienced railroaders intent on recapturing their plundered quarry: they simply pushed the cars onto the next available siding. As a final measure, Andrews set fire to one of his cars, hoping to engulf a covered bridge in flames as he passed under it. Again, he failed.

By this point, the desperate whistle of the pursuers had attracted the attention of Confederate officials and soldiers along the railroad. A perceptive telegraph agent, having noticed a problem with wires to Atlanta, had come across the pursuit in progress and was picked up. He was dropped off in Dalton and immediately sent word of the plot forward to Chattanooga, where Confederate forces were alerted and sent southbound on the railway.

When "the Texas" caught up with "the General" outside Ringgold, the latter was about to give out. Under strict orders to flee, Andrews and his men abandoned the engine and dispersed.

A manhunt began. Within two weeks, all 22 suspects had been captured (some hundreds of miles away) and thrown into a military prison in Chattanooga. Eight of the men escaped in October 1862 and another six were set free in an exchange for Confederate POWs in 1863. The ringleader, Andrews, and the seven other principals were hanged in Atlanta after standing trial and were unceremoniously buried together in an unmarked grave.

Kennesaw House is Marietta's most haunted building, with claims that 700 ghosts have inhabited the former inn.

To the Union, these men were war heroes. Later disinterred and buried with full honors at Chattanooga National Cemetery, they were made recipients, along with their co-conspirators, of the newly created Congressional Medal of Honor.

By 1864 the Union had taken control of Marietta. Fletcher House, which had been used as a Confederate hospital early in the war, now served the same purpose for the Yankees. General Sherman spared the building, it is said, because Fletcher himself was a Mason. Also, the famous commander was aware of Fletcher's son-in-law's Union leanings.

When the war ended, Marietta lay in ruins. Dix Fletcher reopened his hotel in 1867 and named it Kennesaw House. In the 1920s, it became an office and business complex. As the years passed, various businesses and restaurants occupied the property.

In the 1980s Kennesaw House again became an office complex. The Downtown Marietta Development Authority purchased the house in the mid-1990s. Dan Cox, a city councilman, oversaw the renovation of the building and the installation of the Marietta Museum of History on the second floor. He accumulated a fine collection of artifacts, including some that predate European settlement, as well as others that offer a broad portrait of Marietta and its changing fortunes.

So what of the house's ghosts? Rumors that hundreds of ghosts inhabit the historic home are simply false. Yet according to Cox, there's no denying the presence of the paranormal. In 1994 Cox was standing in front of the elevator on the second floor, talking to his wife. Suddenly he felt someone standing beside him. It was a medium-sized man dressed as a doctor in a flat hat, leather boots and a cream-colored linen coat that hung right above his knees. He wore a serious look on his face and seemed to command respect. Before Cox could smile or introduce himself, the man disappeared.

Recalling that the house had been used as a hospital (and morgue) by both sides in the war, Cox wondered if the doctor might be Dr. Wilder, who treated Confederate casualties at Kennesaw House. Or perhaps it was another doctor? After all, at the height of hostilities, many doctors traveled through town to care for the ever-growing numbers of dead and dying soldiers. Kennesaw House simply could not accommodate all the casualties, so bodies were piled up wherever space was available—in homes, schools, public buildings and eventually roadways and fields. Given the high levels of loss and suffering, it should come as little surprise that the ghost of a doctor remained behind as a symbol of Marietta's aid to the Confederate cause. Regardless of his identity, Cox reported that two others have seen the man in the white coat, lending credence to his eyewitness account.

The other prominent "ghost" at Kennesaw House is nothing of the sort: it's an elevator. Cox reported that it spontaneously rises to the second floor and opens its doors when no one is nearby. Sometimes, too, there is a jerking motion during this mysterious activity, almost as if someone is preventing the doors from closing. In any case, whether ghosts or simply a faulty electrical system is behind the elevator's odd behavior, visitors to the museum may want to consider the stairs.

Ezekiel Harris House

Augusta

As a musket ball struck a nearby tree, Tom Glass rushed back to his injured brother's side. Will's gray coat was soaked crimson, and when Tom pulled it open, he saw that the makeshift bandage had staunched the flow of blood. At 15, Tom knew nothing of medicine and very little of war, but he could read the despair in his older brother's eyes. He needed help fast.

"Don't worry, Will. Can you move?"

Will tried to prop himself up with his elbows but fell back. He whispered, "Go, Tom, leave me here, but rout these Loyalist pigs. Don't let me die in vain."

Tom looked at his rusty old musket. He had no ammunition or powder, and his bayonet had snapped off. Will's weapon was nowhere in sight. The patriots' brutal five-day siege of the White House, originally called McKay's Trading Post, a mile outside Augusta, was finally drawing to a close.

Suddenly Tom heard the clumping of heavy boots nearby. He looked back and saw General Elijah Clarke, who had led Augusta's rebellious militia in the marathon assault. As the general stormed past, he shouted desperately, "Glass brothers, retreat now! The battle is lost!"

"General, wait! My brother is wounded!"

But Clarke, once the picture of courage, had already turned tail toward the horses waiting on the other side of the river. Tom glanced back at the battered three-story building, 50 yards away, which they had unsuccessfully laid siege to. As the patriots beat a hasty retreat, Tory sharpshooters were picking them off. If Tom tried to carry Will to the river, they would both be gunned down. But if they surrendered, could they expect clemency? The fighting had been bitter, and there was no love lost on either side.

The fight had meant everything to Tom and Will. Ever since the British took Augusta five years previous, the citizens had been harassed and bullied. Initially the ill treatment came from General Archibald Campbell, the merciless dictator who had captured the city with almost no resistance. His replacement, Colonel Thomas Brown, the leader of the forces now inside the trading post, was even worse. He had revolutionaries beaten and arrested, and burned and pillaged their property.

When the brothers saw Brown's redcoats set fire to their neighbors' barn and slaughter their cattle, they joined the militia. General Clarke had inspired a ragtag band of 300 rebels to take Augusta back. Few had formal military training, but what they lacked in sophisticated maneuvering strategy they more than made up in good old-fashioned bile. In early September 1780, Clarke proposed a siege on the White House. The battle cry that filled the tavern still rang in Tom's ear: "Death to the British dogs! Death to the king!"

Now the much-anticipated showdown between Clarke and Brown was at an end. But as Tom held his helpless brother in his arms, wiping the perspiration off his brow, he didn't think of the fate of Augusta or the Whig cause or even the bitter war that would determine the fate of the colonies. He thought of his beloved brother Will.

Meanwhile, inside the outpost, Colonel Brown observed the scene from an upstairs window with satisfaction. Only yesterday his company was parched, hungry and exhausted, on the brink of ignominious defeat. Some had gone mad

Ezekiel Harris House, before renovations

from the heat and claustrophobia. Yet in spite of their pleas to surrender, he refused them: nothing could make him give up. Then British troops and the Cherokee under Colonel Kruger's command arrived and turned the tide. The rebels were fleeing into the woods, routed and bloodied. This was the moment Brown had sought for nearly five years, not because it represented a key victory for the Loyalists, but because it would present him with an opportunity to smite the Liberty Boys once and for all, to make them pay for a bitter humiliation...

For Colonel Brown, it seemed like only yesterday.

On the morning of October 5, 1775, at the time simply a loyal citizen of King George, Brown had caught a few catfish in the river and was walking along the bank toward Augusta.

Suddenly, a group of men came up from behind him, scattering a pile of autumn leaves.

"Grab the Loyalist bastard!" one of them yelled.

They dragged him into the woods and stripped him, then poured hot tar on him and covered him in pillow feathers, all the while laughing and mocking the British crown. Brown recognized them as the Liberty Boys, a fearless band of revolutionary miscreants he had opposed wherever their paths crossed. After angry words were exchanged outside Wilson's Tavern, an escalation seemed inevitable. Now he was their captive, and they intended to humiliate him.

The Liberty Boys hoisted Brown onto a wagon, shackled him and paraded him along Augusta's main thoroughfare. He was almost unrecognizable under the feathers, so two of his captors marched alongside the wagon, ringing bells and announcing his name. "Behold! We present Thomas Brown, the mightiest rooster in King Georgie Porgie's service!" Throngs of pro-revolutionary onlookers laughed at the shameful spectacle. When it was all over, his captors released him and banished him from Augusta. As he tried to scrape the sticky tar off, the bitter Brown vowed one day to return with a contingent of men to slaughter the insolent rebels.

After five years, that day had finally come.

Marshalling all his anger, Brown shouted out the window, "Traitors to King George III, surrender now or be killed!"

Moments later, the front door of the battered house, barred shut for nearly a week, creaked opened to reveal two Cherokee men holding war hatchets and rusty shackles. Behind them stood a small group of armed redcoats. The braves scanned the battle-scarred yard, then walked out, accompanied by the redcoats. Those patriots who could stand rose and raised their hands to surrender. In a matter of moments, two soldiers had snatched up Tom and Will and dragged them toward the house. When Will groaned in pain and slipped to the ground, they realized he was injured and forced Tom to carry him.

When they got inside, Tom smelled sweat and feces under the fading musk of gunpowder. It was dark and the heat was thick and sticky. He gagged as Loyalist soldiers discussed their exploits, gesturing with their hands, glad of their hard-earned victory. Their joy turned to spite when they caught sight of the prisoners. The entire floor fell silent. Scowls stretched the faces of the Tories, and some spat at the feet of the captives.

The stairs to the second floor creaked as two sets of boots began to descend, burdened by something heavy. Two men carried a chair in which Colonel Brown sat. Although both his thighs were heavily bandaged, with a noticeable seepage of blood on each, he sat confident and upright. A musket lay across his lap.

When he was put down, he stood up tall and defiant, weapon in hand, almost ready to fight if necessary. "Which one of you bastards shot me?"

His eyes filled with spite. He wanted nothing more than to identify the Liberty Boys and to cut their dirty throats. He scanned the faces of the prisoners. Some wore looks of dejection, others defiance, but he recognized none of the 28 captives before him. Brown seethed. Had he been rendered lame and sacrificed everything for king and country only to let his one chance for revenge slip through his fingers?

Suddenly Tom spoke up.

"Sir, my brother is badly injured. Please allow him to quench his thirst."

Brown looked at Will, who was barely able to stand. "Thirst? *Ha!* You don't know the meaning of the word! Old Franklin in the corner there's been on death's doorstep for four days, watching the rot invade his wounds. *Four days!*" he bellowed. "Nothing to eat, nothing to drink, no medicine. We begged and pleaded for some respite, for meager increments of water, for bread. You laughed at us and reloaded your muskets. Having shown us no mercy, now you shall have none yourself!"

At this, Henry Warwick, a British officer, stepped forward. Sensing a breach of protocol, he said, "Colonel, these men cannot be held accountable for the actions of their commanders. They are captives."

"Silence, Lieutenant Warwick! My orders are final. Thirteen of these scoundrels shall be hanged at the house they sought to capture—one for every rebellious colony. The hangings will take place in the stairwell, where I may witness each one. Long live the king!"

At the rear of the house was an open stairwell that rose from the backyard to the second and third stories in a spiral. Colonel Brown returned upstairs and was propped up in his bed so he could watch each execution through a window. One by one, the prisoners met their cruel fates as Brown looked on, smiling.

Tom couldn't see the horrid spectacle from his vantage on the first floor, but he heard the snapping of each neck and the squeaking of the rope against the wood as each body dangled at the end of the noose. Then it was the brothers' turn. Will was too weak to make the trip to the makeshift gallows at the top of the stairs, so Tom carried him once more. As he struggled up the stairs, Tom thought of his mother, Catherine. He remembered the morning he and Will set out.

She ran out the door, pleading with them not to go. Their faces were stone cold, hers hot with tears. She had her duty as a mother; they had theirs as men.

The executioner, a boy no older than Tom, secured the noose around Will's neck. Although nearly unconscious, Will became suddenly aware of his surroundings and gathered the strength to grit his teeth and stand erect. Tom turned away, and Will was gone.

The noose was moist with the sweat of condemned men. The last thing Tom saw was Colonel Brown's face, his eyes fixed. But Tom felt no hate or resentment, only pity that war and spite and hatred had broken his heart.

The remaining 15 captives were turned over to the Cherokee, who took them outside and tortured them to death. The Royal Governor of Georgia, James Wright, made note of the hangings in a report, which, he hoped, would "have a very Good Effect" on the remaining revolutionary element in and around Augusta. As for Brown, he and other commanders loyal to the Crown continued to burn plantations and subjugate the locals. Ultimately, however, they were unsuccessful in getting Georgians to submit to a royal government.

Today, more than 200 years after the executions, Ezekiel Harris House is considered one of the best-preserved 18th-century homes in Georgia. It was renovated and refurnished in 1964 and opened to the public. Many visitors come to the house to appreciate its beauty and learn about Augusta history.

Over the years, visitors have reported many strange sounds in the stairwell. It is said that when visitors close their eyes and count to 13, some can hear the agonizing groans of the patriots as they were hanged. Similar sounds have been reported when the visitors stand on the 13th step.

The house's only ghost never visited the house, but spent much of her adult life trying to put it out of her mind. It is Mrs. Glass, the mother of Tom and Will. Only days before they set off, she had a premonition of their deaths during a dream. Friends tried to keep word of her sons' deaths from her, but eventually she learned of the hangings. She was appalled that they had been executed as pawns in Colonel Brown's bitter plot for revenge. For many months she was inconsolable, distraught beyond grieving.

Her ghost has been seen on the third floor and the staircase of the house, with her face etched in worry, searching in vain for her dead sons. She wears a shimmering white gown and carries a handkerchief in her left hand.

The manager of 1797 Ezekiel Harris House says, "For many years, it was believed that the 1797 Ezekiel Harris and the White House (or Mackay House) were one and the same. With the approach of the country's bicentennial, however, research was conducted that proved that the actual White House was not the Harris House at all."

He says, "The most obvious difference is that the Harris House was built in 1797 and so did not even exist during the Revolutionary War." And "unfortunately, the White House no longer stands—it was mostly destroyed during a Revolutionary War battle known as the First Siege of Augusta."

So the mystery deepens. If the White House and the Harris House were never the same structure, how do we explain the paranormal events in the Harris House? Did the spirits of the patriots move into the Harris House to remind visitors of their tragic end?

The mystery continues...

Fort McAllister

NEAR SAVANNAH

Positioned 12 miles south of Savannah overlooking a place called Genesis Point, Fort McAllister was used in the Civil War to defend the mouth of the Ogeechee River and prevent Union ships from reaching key supply corridors upstream. The fort was able to repel Yankee attacks time and again, largely because of its innovative earthen-mound fortifications. Of course, the fort's defenses could only hold out so long. By the time General Sherman's Union troops overran it in 1864, two valiant Confederates (one of whom was not even a soldier) had given their lives for the cause—and would return later as ghosts.

The fort was constructed in 1861 by slaves on land owned by Joseph L. McAllister, who agreed to let the site be used for military purposes. Unlike nearby Fort Pulaski, a masonry fortification, the architects of Fort McAllister covered over their gun emplacements with sod and fill dredged from the bottom of the Ogeechee River. The fort's firepower consisted of seven emplacements, the most powerful of which was the Columbiad, a large gun capable of hurling 8-inch shells with great accuracy at targets one to three miles away. A complement of 230 soldiers occupied the fort.

After the fall of Fort Pulaski in 1862, Fort McAllister was expected to prevent Union ships from breaking through. To this end, large obstructive "piles" were placed in the river near the fort, allowing only Confederate vessels to cross. Undeterred by this measure, the Union attacked the fort seven times.

The first exchange occurred in July 1862 after the Confederate steamer *Nashville* had sneaked through the Union blockade of Charleston Harbor and was being hotly pursued by the USS *Montauk*. The *Nashville* successfully made it to the Ogeechee mouth and dropped anchor, but the enemy boats quickly set up a blockade and began to shell the fort in an attempt to get at the vessel. They failed, but later mounted another assault in an attempt to destroy the *Nashville*.

In spite of the heavy shelling, the spongy earthen defenses proved remarkably efficient bastions, "swallowing" countless cannonballs. But though Fort McAllister returned any fire it took, the enemy's ironclad boats—another innovation at the time—proved equally resilient. During exchanges, the *Montauk* was struck more than 50 times, but the shells simply ricocheted off of it into the river.

The *Nashville* was eventually sunk as it attempted to break through the blockade, but the fort's defenses ultimately prevented the Union from crippling Confederate supply lines upriver during 1863 and 1864.

Major John B. Gallie was one of the Confederate casualties during the second bombardment in February 1863. A Union ironclad boat, positioned about 800 yards north of the battery, opened fire, hoping to silence the formidable Columbiad. The major was injured by a piece of shrapnel, but he continued to direct the fort's counterattack, refusing to be relieved until another shell hit him directly in the head. Debate exists over whether he was merely scalped or decapitated, but he perished instantly and was greatly mourned by those under his command.

Fort McAllister never surrendered, but it was taken in December 1864. Near the end of his March to the Sea,

General Sherman sent eight battalions to approach the fort by land from the rear. With the fort disabled, he hoped to reach the key supply lines on the river. His 4,000-odd Union troops were forced to navigate a minefield outside the fort, but ultimately overtook it without much difficulty because it was not designed to resist a land assault. Union forces then advanced on Savannah, taking it within a week and bringing an end to Sherman's bloody and decisive campaign.

The fort fell into disrepair after the war. Eventually the industrialist Henry Ford, owner of large holdings in nearby Richmond Hill, set out to restore it in the late 1930s. The site later came into the possession of the state, which returned it to its wartime condition and opened it to the public in 1963, just over 100 years after it was initially attacked. Among the fort's attractions are the Columbiad and other wartime relics, such as the furnace where cannonballs were heated so they could be fired red-hot. The earthen bomb proofs are off limits to visitors because they are susceptible to erosion, but the service magazine, which held the gunpowder, shells and fuses for the 30-pound gun, is available for viewing.

Given the heroic circumstances of his death, it's no surprise that Major Gallie is one of the fort's ghosts. The first sighting took place one mild February day in the 1960s as groundskeepers were trimming the grass near the fort's massive gun. All of a sudden the men were overcome with an icy chill. At first they thought the weather had suddenly shifted, but a quick glance at the sky convinced them that the temperature dip was localized to their environs. Their confusion turned to terror when they spotted a headless ghost near where the major was killed. He wore a Confederate uniform and, although headless, his body was carefully oriented to the sea, almost as if he was still on the lookout for enemy boats. The men immediately fled the scene.

Another sighting took place in 2002 when a man from North Carolina heard some shouting near the same spot. At first he assumed it was a parent trying to discipline a child or a staff member chiding a curious visitor who had ventured onto the fortifications. Ordinarily the man would walk away from such exchanges, feeling embarrassed for the participants, but this one seemed different—almost violent and entirely one-sided. He walked in the direction of the shouting, and as he did he could make out words that sounded like "Fire!" and "More powder!" Then he stopped suddenly near the fort's magazine, having localized the racket. It was a hazy, bright day, but as he squinted he could see a very faint apparition near the Columbiad. It was crouched down, and seemed to be wary of incoming fire from overhead. The man was no expert on Civil War uniforms, but the apparition's outfit seemed more formal than the run-of-the-mill Confederate variety. He tried to approach the ghost, but it disappeared into the muggy air, never to return. The man later asked at the park office about the apparition, and was told about the spirit of Major Gallie. Because the apparition appeared to have his head intact, the man was unsure if the presence was indeed that of the heroic major, but he remained terrified by the encounter for years.

The other ghost at the fort is not human. "Tom Cat," a tenacious coal black cat, served as the fort's mascot—a key distraction during long lulls between action. Despite inevitable associations of bad luck connected to black cats, Tom Cat was loved by the entire garrison. During bombardments, he was said to race along the grassy fortifications dodging heavy artillery fire, and his courage inspired the men.

On March 3, 1863, during a seven-hour bombardment from 10 Union boats, Tom Cat was struck by a cannonball and died instantly. Remarkably enough, he was the only Confederate casualty that day. The following day, General Beauregard was alerted of his death and he was buried with full military honors; today, a plaque commemorates his short life.

The cat's ghost is usually spotted for only several seconds as he darts across the fortification mounds or ducks into one of the buildings. Like Major Gallie, he appears to be still on duty in the afterlife.

One sighting, by a girl in the 1980s, reveals the power of Tom Cat's presence. Jessica Miller, then in the fifth grade at a school outside Atlanta, was visiting the fort on a field trip with her class. Unlike her peers, she considered the field trip to be a genuine learning opportunity, not simply a chance to misbehave on the bus and goof off at the site before returning to the drudgery of Mr. Mackie's homeroom. Upon arrival, she sneaked away from everyone else, eager to envision the fort as it once was. She knew that one of the teachers would eventually notice her absence, track her down and scold her—a well-established pattern—but she didn't care. This visit was probably the only time she'd see a Civil War site, so she was determined to make it memorable by enjoying it on her own terms.

The weather was hot and muggy. Jessica wanted to see the emplacement that held the Columbiad. She found it and scrambled onto the grass that covered it, disobeying the "keep off" signs. Looking over the water, it was not difficult to imagine the scene so many years ago—the pungent smell

Federal soldiers with big gun at Fort McAllister.

of artillery smoke heavy in the air, orders shouted over agonized groans of pain, cannonballs flying through the air, then crushing into pieces whatever they happened to strike. A sudden, unexpected sound interrupted her reverie: the purring of a cat. For a moment, Jessica thought of her own tabby, Petulia, but this cat's purr was unmistakably different—older, more experienced, more *worn.*

"Jessica!" a voice cried out from about 50 feet away. "Mr. Mackie is mad at you!"

Jessica frowned. It was the cloying voice of Carol MacDonald, her nemesis, a girl with thick glasses whose only purpose in life—other than to beat Jessica on spelling tests—was to torment her in every way possible.

Wary of discovery, Jessica dashed into one of the emplacements. It was dark and silent and musty inside, and seemed to smell vaguely of an unknown chemical. She hid right beside the doorway, pressing her back against the dusty wall, and held her breath as Carol approached and poked her nose in. A tense moment passed. Finally Carol turned around and left, and Jessica slowly let out her breath.

But the tension in the dark space somehow remained: Jessica sensed someone or something else nearby. She remained frozen in fear, hoping that whatever it was would leave as Carol had. But her impatience quickly dissipated, especially after her eyes grew accustomed to the darkness, and instead of bolting away, Jessica remained in the emplacement, savoring a deep sensation of calm, of communion, even hoping it would carry on indefinitely. All the while, she heard the light sound of purring.

None of this happened in a vacuum. Jessica was aware that Carol had probably alerted the teachers to her absence, causing a miniature posse to assemble; and she was also aware that the other kids would give her a rough time on the long ride home, as they always did. But it didn't matter. Somehow, inexplicably, she had made a friend.

Jessica was eventually discovered and dragged away by the teacher. But every March 3, on the anniversary of Tom Cat's heroic death, she makes a point to remember her peaceful séance with the most likeable ghost of Fort McAllister.

Fort Pulaski

Cockspur Island

Fort Pulaski on Cockspur Island was completed in 1847. Named for Count Casimir Pulaski, a revolutionary war hero who died during the Siege of Savannah in 1779, the fortification strategically blocked the mouth of the Savannah River leading to the city. Two previous forts stood on the same plot: Fort George, which dates to the middle of the 18th century, and Fort Greene, built in 1794 and destroyed 10 years later by a powerful hurricane.

Fort Pulaski was a formidable masonry garrison that took 18 years to complete. Shaped like a crude hexagon, it was built with more than 25 million local red and gray bricks and featured a moat, casemates and powder magazines. One of the officers who oversaw its construction in the 1830s was a young West Point graduate named Robert E. Lee, who returned, greatly improved in rank, after volunteers from Savannah seized it in 1861. Four months later, the attack on Fort Sumter would begin a chain of events that led to the Civil War.

During the war, the Union tried to block any shipments of supplies to the key port of Savannah. Fort Pulaski helped protect the shipping corridor, allowing weapons and medicine to reach Confederate forces.

In the spring of 1862, Federal troops under the command of Major General David Hunter set up camp, unopposed, on Tybee Island, some 8,000 yards from the fort. The 400 or so Confederates stationed at Fort Pulaski could do nothing but watch from their protected garrison as the enemy erected

View of soldiers and cannon, Fort Pulaski

36 heavy experimental cannon, including 10 Parrott rifles capable of firing 30-pound shells over long distances.

On the morning of April 10, after the Confederate Colonel Charles H. Olmstead had refused to surrender, the artillery barrage began. Within hours the enormous Yankee shells had blown a sizable hole in the fort's southeastern wall; under additional fire, the wall was reduced to rubble. Olmstead was in a bind, lacking any comparable artillery power and unable to launch a counterattack. The heavy shelling continued into the next day. When rounds began to land near the highly explosive powder magazines, the colonel was forced to surrender before losing a single man. Olmstead laid down his sword with the words, "I yield my sword. I trust I have not disgraced it."

It would become the first in a series of Yankee bombardments that would spell the end of masonry fortifications across the South.

Near the end of the war, from October 1864 to March 1865, Fort Pulaski was used as a prison for approximately 550 Confederate POWs. As in many prison camps during the war, conditions were almost inhuman. The Union felt its own prisoners of war had been poorly treated by the Confederates, so the rebel captives at Fort Pulaski were left to suffer. During the unusually grim winter of 1864–65, the prisoners were incarcerated in unheated steel casemates and given little to eat. Pneumonia and scurvy quickly spread through the ranks. By the war's end, 13 men had died in captivity and were unceremoniously buried in unmarked graves outside the fort.

The fort slowly fell into disrepair until it was declared a national monument and restored in the 1930s. Open to the public, the fort now offers tours of its casemates and stages summertime historical recreations in which participants dress up in uniforms from the 1860s and stage artillery drills. But it seems that the fort's ghosts are also interested in keeping the past alive.

One of the best-known paranormal accounts was told by a former staff member named Josh. The summer before starting work at the fort, he and a friend, looking for something fun to do, arrived at Cockspur Island one night with a metal detector. It was around midnight and the two assumed the place was deserted. As they walked through the tall grass outside the fort, both men got the feeling that someone else was present. Josh turned off the metal detector and flashlight, and both listened carefully. They thought that maybe a security guard had noticed their boat and come to investigate.

Both men froze when they heard footsteps on the other side of a large bush. But soon after they froze, the footsteps—which sounded heavy, like an adult male's—stopped too. By this point, they were terrified. Was someone following them? Desperate to find out, Josh motioned his friend to keep walking to the edge of the bush, certain that they could then see whoever was there. But when they turned the corner, there was no one! The footsteps were fleeing toward the marsh, now rather loudly, but the men could see nothing, not even after Josh turned his flashlight back on. Scared out of their minds, both turned tail and headed for their boat.

As it happened, the experience became a pivotal moment in Josh's life. He studied the U.S. Civil War in college, learning a lot about the fort while working there, and eventually became a public relations assistant. He never could have imagined that a silly teenage lark would one day become his life's work.

During his time at the fort, the man avoided going near the casemates. He said he never saw a presence there, but feelings of desperation and suffering permeated the area. He noted that the detail about no man dying during the artillery barrage was not entirely accurate. Following the surrender, a man did die from an injury sustained during the attack. The stairway where he stood watch is said to arouse feelings of pity and anger.

Several sighting of ghosts have been reported at Fort Pulaski. One dates back to World War II. A woman and her

Prisoners were incarcerated in unheated casemates near the end of the war.

husband had been walking along Tybee Beach when they noticed a number of soldiers walking along the top of the walls at the fort.

Did the sighting involve real soldiers being trained for the war effort? It's hard to say.

Another sighting happened early one morning in 1965. A man on vacation from Atlanta had taken a boat from Tybee to Cockspur Island. He was interested in watching birds and identifying certain species of flowers. As he rummaged around, he saw something colorful in the distance by one of the walls of the fort. He approached the item, assuming it was a wildflower. As he got closer, however, it looked more and more like a bloodstained piece of gauze. When he was about 50 yards away, he heard the cry of a bird overhead. Almost instinctively, he brought his binoculars up to his eyes to see what it was. Recognizing the bird's cry, he correctly identified it as a relatively rare marsh bird. He was proud that his keen powers of observation allowed him to spot it mid-flight. When the bird had flown out of view, the man turned back to the strange object by the wall. But it was gone. After a thorough investigation he found nothing, apart from what he remains convinced was a dried blood stain on the wall.

A bona fide ghost sighting took place in the mid-1990s. A mother and her son needed to find the washrooms at the fort, so they approached a sentry. They complimented him on the uniqueness of his uniform and saber, then asked about the restrooms. The sentry replied that he could not leave his post to point them out.

The pair wandered around and eventually found a park ranger. He told them that the restrooms were near the front entrance, and that he'd be happy to show her. The mother

Specters of soldiers have been spotted walking along Tybee Beach.

got annoyed at this, telling the ranger about the sentry in the uniform who said that he couldn't leave his post.

"A sentry in uniform?" the ranger replied. "We don't have soldiers dressed in uniforms here, ma'am."

"But we both met and talked to him," the boy said.

Sensing something unusual, the three quickly returned to the spot where they had met the sentry. He had vanished without a trace.

Taken together, the ghost stories at Fort Pulaski don't point to a single spirit. Rather, they reveal an environment of lingering despair and pain, many years after Confederate prisoners were so unfairly imprisoned in the fortification they once controlled.

3
Historical Haunts

The Springer Opera House
COLUMBUS

Francis Joseph Springer, a native of Alsace in Northern Europe, came to Columbus before the Civil War and made his fortune as a grocery entrepreneur. He watched with interest as the city planned to construct a theater for the performing arts. Columbus had shown an appetite for theater since its earliest days.

The outbreak of the war interrupted the plans, but he took them up again in the late 1860s when backers began to raise money and select a site. Springer became a key player in the history of the theater that would take his family name. A devotee of the arts, he graciously allowed his store, on one of the busiest corners in Columbus, to be demolished so the new European-style theater could go up in its place. Springer pledged a sizeable amount of the money for the construction with the understanding that the ownership would pass over to him and his heirs.

The theater opened on February 21, 1871. As Restoration buildings go, it was quite elaborate. Made of bricks, it rose to three stories, had red plush seats, gilded fixtures and was illuminated by fine gas lamps. It soon became the most talked-about theater in Georgia. Audiences from across the South arrived in expensive coaches to watch sold-out performances. If they desired, they could even stay in the Springer Hotel, which was situated on the upper floors.

Over the next 50 years, many celebrities took to the Springer's grand stage including Ethel Barrymore, Will Rogers, Ruth Gordon and P.T. Barnum's diminutive General

Tom Thumb. The composer Irving Berlin and the band leader John Philip Sousa both appeared at the Springer, as did famous orators such as William Jennings Bryan, Oscar Wilde and Franklin D. Roosevelt.

It couldn't last. As with many great 19th-century theaters, the Great Depression of the 1930s spelled the end of a golden age of performing arts. The road companies that once ferried show caravans across the nation suddenly tightened their belts, and a new player in the entertainment game, motion pictures, slowly replaced the great stage acts of the early 20th century. By the 1940s, the theater had been transformed into a movie house; by the early 1960s, as downtown Columbus slumped economically, so did the Springer. In 1963 it was slated for demolition.

Only the efforts of some determined citizens saved the old theater. It was subsequently restored, and reopened in 1965 with a performance of a play adapted from a novel by local writer Augusta Jane Evans Wilson.

In 1998 the state spent $12 million to usher the Springer Opera House into the 21st century. Formerly closed areas were expanded into public spaces, and state-of-the-art sound and lighting systems were installed. Wherever possible, the restorers took pains not to replace or disturb priceless original features. The result was a world-class institution with a timeless appeal that proudly serves today as the State Theater of Georgia.

The Springer shows classic and contemporary plays by famous theater companies, and famous performers of all kinds once again tread on its deep stage. The theater is also home to a drama school for young actors, the Springer Theater Academy, one of the most prestigious of its kind in

Over the years, staff have reported many unexplained occurrences in the theater.

the United States, and a small museum that presents a history of the theater.

While the future looks bright for the Springer, the past remains a key element of its appeal, not only because of its tradition of theatrical excellence, but because of its ghosts, too.

Over the years, staff have reported many unexplained occurrences. Mysterious music has played in the darkened theater, props have been moved with no explanation and stage lights, which can only be dimmed or brightened, have been known to blink on and off. Once, many pairs of shoes from the prop room were discovered on a staircase, set up to look as if they were ascending. A pair of cowboy boots at the top appeared to vanish into a wall. While staff at the theater say the disturbances are extremely rare, and there's no guarantee that ghosts are behind them, there's no denying that not everything is as it seems at the historic theater.

Even audience members have had unusual encounters. A man named Robert Carrollton, for instance, was sitting in one of the theater's boxes when he heard a noise behind the box door. When he looked over, he saw a gentleman watching the play. Carrollton reported that looking into the man's eyes sent a cold shiver through his body. Intrigued, he got up to talk with the man, who was dressed in an old-fashioned outfit that looked vaguely theatrical. But the man vanished immediately, leaving only a musty smell behind.

Perhaps the theater's roster of celebrities has something to do with all the mysterious activity. After all, many theaters in America become haunted by spirits of famous actors or directors.

If the Springer has a resident ghost, it would be Edwin Booth, best remembered today as the brother of another famous actor, John Wilkes Booth, who shot and killed President Abraham Lincoln in 1865.

For a year after the assassination, Edwin did not perform. He worried that audiences would think of him only as the brother of the presidential assassin. A critically acclaimed performance of *Hamlet* in the Winter Garden Theater in New York in 1866 convinced everyone otherwise; he was a force unto himself.

Booth set out on a Southern tour in 1876. Since he still had some friends in Columbus and knew the reputation of the Springer Opera House, he planned to stop in the city. When the manager of the theater, John Burrus, responded energetically to one of his letters, the actor resolved to play his most famous role.

The first performance took place on February 15, 1876. In his inky velvet cloak, Booth held the audience enraptured with his presentation of the Danish prince. For years following, those in attendance bragged, much as contemporary audiences might about a rock star, that they had seen Booth play Hamlet.

According to some eyewitnesses, Booth continues to perform at the Springer—not on stage but in the costume area, and not as an actor but as a mischievous specter.

One of the most prominent encounters took place late one night in the 1970s. At the time, a heavy metal door separated the costume area from the rest of backstage. A single key, kept in one of the offices, was to be used only by authorized personnel. When a theater staff member noticed it was missing, she made a thorough search of the office but turned up nothing. Then she went by to investigate, and found the door securely locked.

When she returned to the office, the key was waiting in its appointed place on the desk. But no one had left the building or entered, so the question was, who put the key back?

The woman, by this time a little frustrated but happy to be in possession of the key she needed, walked back to the costume area. When she arrived at the door, she noticed that the lock had been opened and the hasp was swinging back and forth. Someone must have been there only moments

Edwin Booth in his critically acclaimed role as Hamlet.

before, but since she had been holding the key for several minutes, who could it have been?

With her curiosity piqued and a few hairs standing on end, she walked into the costume area. The racks were in disarray and one of the trunks had been opened and rummaged through. After a careful inspection of the costumes, the woman determined that the intruder had been searching for costumes from *Hamlet*. But why? It was not being performed or even under consideration. One explanation pointed at Booth's ghost, who was showing his frustration with the Springer for failing to revive the play on which he based his sizable reputation.

Hay House

MACON

Unlike other Georgia magnates of his day, William Butler Johnston made his fortune in banking, railroads and utilities, not cotton. In 1851 Johnston married Anne Clark Tracy, 20 years younger than himself, and the couple set off on an extended honeymoon in Italy. While away, they fell in love with Italian architecture and art and arranged for expensive materials (such as Carrera marble mantles and massive front doors) to be shipped to the United States in preparation for the construction of an extravagant home.

If the home on Georgia Street stands out as one of the finest in the South, it's because the Italian Renaissance Revival was not nearly as popular as the antebellum Greek Revival style. Designed by a New York architect and requiring four years of construction before its completion in 1859, the plan used many symmetrical circular elements (such as the window frames) in place of the Greek style's hard angles. The European extravagance earned the house the name "the Palace of the South," a deserving epithet for a four-story structure occupying some 18,000 square feet. It has 24 rooms and modern amenities such as hot and cold running water, a 15-room speaker tube system and an elaborate ventilation system. The decorative two-story octagonal cupola served as a kind of chimney for the ventilation system, allowing hot air to rise up and pass through it. The equally well-appointed grounds were significantly enhanced by subsequent owners, but some of the surviving gingko trees, cedars and magnolias were among the Johnstons' original plantings.

Hay House, designed in the Italian Renaissance Revival style, is one of the finest homes of the South.

The interior was as impressive as the façade. Furnishings collected during the Johnstons' travels reflected their exquisite taste, as did pieces of art from many world cultures, including valuable paintings on display in the elegant Picture Gallery. An entire room was devoted to their most treasured piece, "Ruth Gleaning," a marble statue of the Biblical figure by celebrated American sculptor Randolph Rogers. Given the extravagances of the home, it is little surprise that it was the center of Macon society as the site of many galas and parties.

The Johnstons' beautiful home, however, couldn't prevent a string of tragedies as the couple tried to start a family. Their first four children died young, and Anne spent many months in seclusion grieving. She emerged rarely, clad entirely in black.

Eventually the war came to Macon. Jefferson Davis, President of the Confederacy, was among the guests who called at the house. Because Johnston held a high post in the Macon depository, he was charged with storing large amounts of Confederate gold in his cellars. Some estimate that he once concealed as much as $1.5 million in bullion, the second-largest cache in the entire South.

Sherman bypassed Macon on his March to the Sea, sparing the Johnstons' house and many other historic properties. However, in the final days of the war, Union General James H. Wilson attacked Macon from the south with cannon and artillery fire. Two cannonballs were fired on the house but miraculously landed in the yard, leaving large craters that were filled only in the last 15 years.

The house once again became a social center after the war and remained so after the passing of Mr. and Mrs. Johnston in 1896. Their daughter, Ellen Tracy, the sixth child (and only one of two to survive) then lived there with her husband, William H. Felton; their son William sold the house in 1926. The next family to occupy the house was the Hay family. Parks Lee Hay, founder of the Banker's Health and Life Insurance Company, and his wife redecorated the mansion to keep up with the changing times, although they could only do so much to maintain its grandeur.

A foundation formed after Mrs. Hay's death in 1962 ensured that the house would be kept up as a museum. It was declared a National Historic Landmark in 1974, and in 1977 the Georgia Trust for Historic Preservation set up the property as a museum and cultural events center. An extensive renovation began in 1980.

It was during this renovation that some mysterious events took place. Workmen saw apparitions on a regular basis, and unusual noises repeatedly interrupted their work. The spirits seemed curious about all the commotion, but have never been identified. The sightings were reported by Fran La Farge, a former director of the museum and therefore a credible witness. La Farge also reported a mysterious presence while she was alone in the house late at night. As she sat doing paperwork in the dining room, La Farge was hit by a blast of hot air, almost as if the door of a hot oven had just been opened. At the same time, she sensed another person in the room, although no one was visible. Another encounter involved a maid who saw a shimmering apparition of a woman in the main hallway while cleaning up. According to La Farge, the maid noticed the ghost's intricately braided hair—a possible giveaway of her identity, as Anne Tracy Johnston often wore such braids. From that day forward, the maid insisted that she work with a companion.

The most well-known haunting at Hay House involves a butler who broke his silence about a ghost in a story by Terri K. Smith in the *Macon Telegraph* in 1984.

Chester Davis was a devoted servant in the Hay household for 29 years, never once breaking protocol or revealing any of the family's secrets. When La Farge came forward with her ghost stories, he followed suit, although he had never

She sensed another person in the room, although no one was visible.

before wanted to tell anyone about what he saw for fear he would be ridiculed.

Davis appears to have seen three separate ghosts on three separate occasions. The first one appeared during the day before a party was to take place that evening. Davis was shining the silver doorknobs in the dining room when he saw a gentleman. "He had on blue pants, a white shirt and looked like he was about 55 years old," Davis said. "He had an open collar like mine, and his hair was pepper gray. He had a real nice haircut—not a hippy haircut—and it was slightly parted in the center." Davis sensed that the man wanted to ask him something, like what was he doing. He looked away for a second and when he looked back the man had disappeared.

Some suspect that the ghost was that of Judge William H. Felton, the tall, distinguished gentleman who married the Johnston's daughter Ellen. His appearance would seem fitting because he liked to entertain in his home and would have been curious about the upcoming party.

A second ghost described in the story appeared one day near the front door around noon. Davis described her as "an elderly white lady…in her 60s, wearing a long blue and white checked dress." Her wide-brimmed straw hat gave Davis the feeling that she had just been at work in the garden. When the woman approached the door and moved to press the doorbell, Davis got up to answer it but no one was there.

A final ghost appeared the very next day on the front lawn near the driveway. Davis said she was in her late 30s or early 40s and wore a netted dress. "It was flimsy and on the purple side," he continued, "kind of light purple, not a deep violet like the flower. She had a hat sitting kind of sideways that matched the dress." As with the others, she disappeared just as quickly as she had materialized.

The identities of these two apparitions remain unclear, but some speculate that the woman on the lawn was the ghost of Luisa McGill Gibson, the wife of William Felton, Jr. After the couple married they lived in the house for a while with William's parents.

Chester Davis made these sightings, but as a paranormal skeptic he doubted their validity until his dying day. The details he provided, however, seem too vivid to be fictional. Although staff at the museum and most Macon residents remain firm in their denials of ghosts at the house, all the different mysterious happenings over the years seem to indicate that there's more to Hay House than meets the eye.

The Homestead

MILLEDGEVILLE

Every homeowner fears it: being awakened on the first night in a new house by loud noises, the kind you'd never notice during the day. In this case, it was a man who had just bought a historic Milledgeville property known as the Homestead from his relatives. On the night in question, he awoke and walked to the window. What he saw baffled him.

An old-fashioned horse-drawn carriage had pulled up to the front of the house. Ladies and gentlemen stepped out, clad in clothing dating back to the mid-19th century, then approached the house. Oil lamps stood along the walkway, illuminating the wooden fence and stairs that led up to the house. The man knew that the entranceway once had these features, having seen them in old photographs, but they had long since been replaced by stone equivalents. Suddenly a woman on the lawn burst out laughing. Everyone fell silent for a moment, then the sounds of the 20 or so congregants resumed, a little louder this time.

The man screwed up his eyes, reminding himself that the year was 1969. True, young people were dressing a bit weird these days, letting their hair grow a lot longer than he preferred, but those gathered outside seemed like they were from another *time*, not just another generation.

Eager to learn more, the man began to descend the stairs. When he reached the landing, he heard a champagne bottle being uncorked and noticed that a party was in full swing in his living room. Couples danced on a polished expanse of floor to the sound of fiddle music, while servants handed out glasses of wine and what looked like caviar. The man recognized no one, and yet it all felt vaguely familiar to him.

Thinking of his relatives, some of the city's leading socialites from the 19th century, the man wondered if someone had decided to throw him a surprise housewarming party. Perhaps, he thought, but why (or how) had the layout and even the furnishings of the first floor been changed? He had spent the entire day moving his own furniture into the place and he hadn't heard so much as a peep before going to bed, so it simply didn't make sense.

A woman's voice snapped him out of his reverie. He looked to the bottom of the stairs and noticed a beautiful lady beckoning him down. Thin and elegant, she wore a striking blue evening gown and a delicate shawl, which partially covered an expensive-looking pearl necklace. Even though he had no idea what era her clothing reflected, he could tell she wore the latest fashions. Her hair was pulled up in a bun, held with a brooch pin, and her eyes shone in the flickering candlelight coming from the elaborate chandeliers.

The man descended, unsure of what to expect, but curious all the same. Suddenly it occurred to him that he was clad in only his bathrobe! But when he looked down, he noticed that he had on a silk dressing gown, expensive shoes and even an ascot. His hair, typically left to its own devices, had been slicked back with some gel-like substance, and he could feel mustache wax on his upper lip. He didn't need to look into a mirror to know that he looked good, and, being the spontaneous type, he just went along with the bizarre scenario.

The woman began to introduce him to the guests at the party. As the man tried to remember all the names, he noticed the strange way in which the people talked, without pauses or "uhs" or "you knows"—almost as if they were summa cum laude graduates of a finishing school somewhere. The interior of the home was no less foreign, since nothing was from the 20th century. The furniture seemed unbearably heavy and cumbersome, and all the wall hangings were oil paintings, not prints, mostly portraits of wealthy sitters. It seemed as if he was in a meticulously restored home, complete with historical reenactors, only everything was genuine.

The man took it all in stride. His escort got his name right and she seemed to be a dear friend, but he couldn't shake the suspicion that it was all a dream. Her incomparable beauty seemed to confirm as much. He had never met a woman so alluring and sophisticated. Yet in spite of his subtle questioning, she revealed very little about the year or her identity; she was more inclined to discuss her successes at piano recitals in Charleston or the latest novels from Great Britain.

The party lasted well into the night—or at least as late as parties so long ago might last. Around 11 PM the guests started to stream out. The man's enchantress, whose name was Amelia, greeted everyone as they left to climb into their carriages waiting outside.

When everyone was gone the man wandered over to the woman, who was directing some servants outside the kitchen door. She took him by the arm and smiled. "What an evening," she said, sighing. He agreed, then began to help with the clean up. Wandering over to the window, he looked out and saw the deserted street in the front of the house. It was unusually dark, so he pulled the curtains closed. It was the last thing he saw. He woke up the next morning on the couch, and everything was back as it should have been—except that the memory of the woman's face had been burned into his mind.

For several weeks following the vision, the man dismissed the entire episode as a dream, attributing the precise details to research he had done on the house before buying it. But one day, as he flipped through some old photos in the public library, he found an image from the 1850s with a familiar face. It was the woman who had enchanted him that night. The man became obsessed with discovering her identity, but was unsuccessful even after carefully combing city records for anyone with the name Amelia. But he never saw her again, nor was there ever another case of retrocognition (as it is called) in the house.

This incident is only one of many that have been reported at the Homestead, a key gathering place for Milledgeville's elite even after the capital changed to Atlanta.

The house was constructed in 1818 by Peter J. Williams for his new bride, Lucinda Parke. A number of prominent Williamses lived in the house, most notably Sue Williams, Peter and Lucinda's beautiful red-haired daughter. Sue's husband, "Honest Jack" Jones, lost his sanity in the house and died after jumping out of a second-story window. Honest Jack's ghost has been spotted on repeated occasions over the years, hovering outside the window where he jumped to his death.

Perhaps the most interesting sightings at the Homestead involve a banshee, the Welsh name for a spirit whose appearance coincides with the death of a loved one. The Williamses, who were originally from Wales, believed that the spirit accompanied them when they immigrated to America.

According to most accounts, the Homestead's banshee is an elderly woman dressed entirely in gray. She is not threatening in the least, or even eerie for that matter. Like a casket bearer at a funeral procession, she walks somberly and deliberately, without facial expression, carrying the weight of sorrow that will inevitably rest on the shoulders of those who spot her.

Her first appearance occurred in the house garden during the Civil War. Several people saw her, and at first they considered her a ghost of some sort—until word came the next day that one of the Williams sons had been killed in combat. The next sighting was many years later, in the 1920s, when a relative of the family, Fanny Ferguson, spotted the reclusive banshee in the back yard. She knew immediately that her sister had passed away.

A final sighting took place in the 1960s. A family friend saw her exit one of the upstairs bedrooms and descend to the first floor. He followed very cautiously as she left the house, walked to Washington Street and eventually headed in the direction of the Memory Hill Cemetery, where she vanished without a trace. No report of a subsequent death was made because the eyewitness couldn't believe his eyes and didn't relate the story until much later. It was only when a member of the family told him of the banshee that the incident made sense to him.

Taken together, the ghostly sightings at the Homestead make it one of Milledgeville's most interesting haunts. Be warned, however: the house is a private residence, so please be sure not to disturb the current residents.

Beall House
MACON

The Beall House was home to Nathan Beall, a tycoon who owned plantations in Sandersville and Hancock County (aside from other holdings). Beall occupied the home with his wife Martha and their children, George and Juliet. Like many families, theirs was changed irreversibly by the Civil War.

In March 1862, George enlisted as a private in the 47th Regiment of the Georgia Infantry. He reported for duty and sent a steady stream of letters home. When these ended in 1863, the Bealls feared the worst, but never got word of their son's death. He had simply disappeared, another casualty of war.

Juliet had married a young local doctor, George C. Griffin, in 1861. Griffin served as an assistant surgeon in the Confederate Army and was sent to Virginia. When he was recalled to Macon for duty in September 1863, he mysteriously disappeared along the way and was never again seen alive. Juliet was shattered, but refused to accept that he was gone. She would sit in a second-story bedroom looking out the window to the road, hoping for her husband's safe return. He never came.

Nathan Beall's wife had also recently died, but he had little time to mourn: his cotton plantations were burned and pillaged toward the end of the war.

With only he and his daughter left in the oversize mansion, Beall decided to sell it. Leonidas A. Jordan, by far the richest man in Macon, bought it for the then-exorbitant sum of $30,000. Yankee soldiers briefly occupied the house as the war wrapped up; then Jordan moved in. Beall and Juliet, meanwhile, moved into a smaller house in town, and finally had time to grieve over their shared wartime losses.

Jordan was an extremely successful railroad tycoon whose vast fortune was worth millions. A noted philanthropist, he contributed greatly to the local performing arts with large endowments to the Macon Opera and the Macon Academy of Music.

His wife, Julia Hurtt Colquitt, was a striking beauty. After marrying, the Jordans lived for many happy years in the former Beall house until Julia fell ill while away on a trip and died of pneumonia on December 30, 1891. Deprived of his love, Jordan lost some of his will to live and his health deteriorated.

But the once-tragic void in his life was filled, it seemed, by a 21-year-old named Ilah Dunlap, who bore an uncanny resemblance to Julia when she was the same age. In spite of his weakened state, Jordan became infatuated with the headstrong beauty. But how could a man of such advanced years, and generally poor health, woo a pretty young thing such as she?

He didn't have to. Dunlap was, in today's lingo, a gold digger. With no money of her own and aware that Jordan had no children, she was able to feign love for the elderly millionaire. In 1893, shortly before the couple wed, Jordan signed over all his holdings to Dunlap. They took a honeymoon tour of Europe with the Dunlap family in tow, staying in expensive hotels and living in the lap of luxury.

For the next six or seven years, Jordan's health declined and he was often close to death. From all indications, the end couldn't come fast enough for Dunlap, who forbade any visitors to their home, including her husband's friends of many years, even as he approached death. It's possible that Dunlap worried that visitors might encourage him to withhold his fortune from her at the eleventh hour.

Jordan died alone in the house in 1899. Dunlap quickly shifted gears, doing everything in her power either to remove reminders of him from her inherited holdings or to play down the source of her enormous fortune. She saw to it, for instance, that Jordan's gravestone in Macon Hill Cemetery was a simple county marker, undeserving of a man of accomplishments and great wealth. By contrast, Dunlap's extravagant marble mausoleum, tellingly inscribed with only her maiden name, became the largest memorial in the entire area. And if that weren't enough, Dunlap began to sell off some of Jordan's family heirlooms, fixtures and furnishings. Without thinking twice, she put everything on the auction block and sold it to the highest bidders.

So completely did Dunlap distance herself from her husband that many people thought her wealth was, in fact, entirely of her own making. Such was the case with officials at the University of Georgia. Dunlap made a large donation to the university near the end of her life, which occasioned the construction of the Ilah Dunlap Library, where her portrait and some other personal articles were put on permanent display. She neglected to mention Leonidas Jordan as the true benefactor, and the university was never the wiser.

The house was the last item to go, sold by Dunlap's brother, who added the distinctive Greek Revival columns and veranda, part of the home's most recognizable details. Today the historic home has been remodeled into a restaurant known as the Bealls 1860 restaurant.

Given Dunlap's inexcusable self-promotion, it would not be surprising if Jordan's ghost came back to upset things in the house where he once lived: he certainly would be justified. The restaurant staff openly admit to some unexplainable phenomena, but it may be that a different spirit—perhaps even a poltergeist—is the resident presence.

One of the most baffling incidents involved a large brown stain that would not go away. Many years ago, although it's not clear exactly when, a woman jumped to her death from a second-floor window. The stain left from her fall—about two feet wide with splatters around it—remains on the concrete to this day. Over the years, staff used bleach, solvents and other cleaners to remove the stain. Initially it comes out, but with time, without fail, it reappears just as it was. Regardless of its origins, the stain remains a persistent reminder of the suffering at Beall House.

While it's possible the suicidal woman is the spirit of the house, some other mysterious activity, much of it mischievous in nature, seems to point toward a more malevolent entity.

One day, a waiter was making some drinks with ice cubes. All of a sudden the cubes jumped out of the glasses and into the air. They dropped to the floor but kept moving around, almost like Mexican jumping beans.

A similarly eerie incident occurred in a small room upstairs, thought to be Jordan's study during his life. According to eyewitnesses, books on the bookshelves would simply fall to the floor without warning and pile up. The frequency became so great that management eventually removed all the books permanently.

Another disturbance, of much greater magnitude, seemed to point at a truly malevolent entity. In 1993 all the pipes in the building started shaking violently. Eventually the entire building began to tremble, and the noise was so earsplitting that the waiters on duty thought there was an earthquake underway. No reasonable explanation was forthcoming, so staff could point only to an otherworldly source.

So what can we conclude about Beall House? Is all the activity perhaps attributable to the ghost of Leonidas Jordan, expressing his afterlife disdain for Ilah Dunlap? Or perhaps he is mourning the loss of his beloved Julia? It's also possible that the spirit of another resident is responsible for the persistent melancholy, such as Juliet or Nathan Beall, who both endured their share of wartime grief. A final possibility, and arguably the strongest, is that an unknown poltergeist inhabits the house and takes pleasure in playing tricks on the restaurant staff. Whatever the case, Beall House remains one of the most fascinating and puzzling haunted properties in Georgia.

Panola Hall

EATONTON

Mr. Nelson froze in his tracks. A woman of incomparable beauty was descending the stairs. She wore an elegant gown, and her curled locks danced as she navigated the stairs with her tiny hand grasping the rail. The flustered businessman stood on the landing and removed his hat, eager to show some courtesy to this charming Southern belle. She passed him nonchalantly, paying him little heed and waving her fan effortlessly. Before he could comment, she had disappeared.

Nelson floated to the top of the stairs, suddenly unaware of where he was or why. Something about the woman left him awestruck. Was it her alabaster skin? The red rose in her hair? Or perhaps the graceful swishes of her old-fashioned hoop-skirted dress? Intent on learning her identity, he rushed downstairs to find her. He searched everywhere on the first floor of Panola Hall in Eatonton, where he was staying as a guest of the Hunt family, but she was nowhere in sight. Only the sweet smell of her rose perfume lingered.

Returning to his room, Nelson tried to focus on his work: namely, setting up a cooperative creamery with the help of Dr. Hunt. As he crunched some numbers and imagined how best to approach the bank, he couldn't shake the vision of the beautiful stranger. To clear his head, he took out some stationery and drafted a letter to his wife and children back home in Ohio. With as much elegance as a serious businessman can muster, Nelson wrote about his delightful train ride and the sophisticated pastimes of his gracious hosts. Eatonton, he continued, was a beautiful little town between

Athens and Macon where flowers grew everywhere and the people seemed very friendly. As he wrote, Nelson suppressed a powerful desire to describe his run-in with the mysterious woman. In fact, he felt deeply inspired to write something— anything—about the strange woman so that he could create a lasting memory of her.

Later that evening over dinner, Nelson mentioned the woman to the Hunts. "I saw someone on the stairs today," he said casually, attempting to downplay his fascination, "but I lost my manners and forgot to introduce myself. May I know who she was?"

The Hunts stared at each other knowingly. Nelson noticed them and wondered why. Was she their maid or perhaps a visitor like him? Did Dr. Hunt have an illegitimate daughter? Although the Hunts appeared to be the sole occupants of Panola Hall, it seemed possible that another person could live in one of the 13 rooms. But why hadn't the Hunts alerted him to her presence? And why wasn't another place set at the dinner table?

"Do you believe in ghosts, Mr. Nelson?" asked Dr. Hunt suddenly.

"Why, no, of course not!" Nelson exclaimed. "We are rational men, are we not? The only ghosts I know appear in novels!"

"I see," Dr. Hunt said. "What if I told you that you saw one today?"

"Why, I…I…I would be left speechless."

The Hunts proceeded to tell Nelson all about Sylvia: when she was most prone to appear, what she wore, who they suspected she was and so forth. Nelson listened, enraptured, although he didn't believe a word. As he saw it, no one so real, so *solid*, could possibly be a ghost.

Over the following days, Nelson waited for Sylvia to reappear, but she didn't. On his final morning in town, desperate to see her again, he waltzed through the house calling her name. Nothing. Then, as he bade the Hunts farewell, he once again smelled the perfume he had first noticed on the staircase. He was again bewitched, and the memory of Sylvia and her sweet fragrance continued to haunt him for a long time.

Sylvia is the resident ghost of Panola Hall on North Madison Avenue in Eatonton, Georgia. The Greek Revival house was built by Henry Trippe and Elizabeth Perry in 1854. Its rooms are spacious and simple, and it has tall Doric columns on its façade. Huge nine-foot windows let in the midday sun while residents can keep warm on cold nights in front of the home's many fireplaces—one in every major room.

The Hunts moved into the Putnam County house in 1876. Dr. Benjamin Hunt, originally from New York, was a man of many talents. A businessman as well as a scientist and amateur horticulturalist, he brought the first Jersey cow to Georgia and built the Peach State's first silo. In 1922 he was awarded an honorary degree in botany from the University of Georgia. Some of the experimental flora he planted around the house can still be seen today.

Hunt's wife, Louise Reid Pruden of Eatonton, was a sophisticated Southerner with exquisite taste and a knack for writing elegant verse. Louise and Dr. Hunt met at a hotel in New York City. After Hunt visited his intended on several occasions, the two married and settled in Eatonton. The Hunts carried out some Victorian renovations on the property and named it Panola Hall.

Although neither had any idea that their house was inhabited by a mysterious ghost, they quickly learned to live in peace with her. The first sighting occurred not long after the happy couple moved in. While reading in the parlor, Mrs. Hunt looked up and saw a shimmering vision of a woman in a full-skirted white dress. Shocked by the intruder, she tried to talk to her, but the vision quickly disappeared. It was the first of many brief encounters.

Being a bit of a romantic, Mrs. Hunt was charmed by the ghost's presence and gave her the name "Sylvia," although for reasons unknown. She also named the upstairs bedroom where the ghost dwelt "Sylvia's Lair." Panola Hall was large and sometimes lonely, and Louise was soothed by the calming presence of the beautiful young spirit. Mrs. Hunt also wrote a verse about her:

> Sylvia's coming down the stair,
> Pretty Sylvia, young and fair.
> Oft and oft I meet her there,
> Smile on lips and rose in hair.

For his part, Dr. Hunt was known to recite his wife's verses, but as a level-headed scientist committed to rational inquiry, he was reluctant to acknowledge the existence of the paranormal. He and his wife downplayed word of their ghostly roommate to others in Eatonton, so very few locals learned of Sylvia's existence. Yet in spite of their discretion, word inevitably got out. After all, Eatonton was a small town, and in small towns one person's business has a way of becoming another's.

One beautiful evening, Alice Wardwell, the town librarian, was returning to the library to reopen it after dinner. Eatonton's library was right across from Panola Hall, so she occasionally looked over into the Hunts' place, either on her way to work or after locking up at night. Both Dr. Hunt and his wife were loyal patrons of the library.

On this occasion, Miss Wardwell stepped outside to smoke a cigarette and escape the heat inside. From where she stood, she could clearly see the couple through a lit window. Both were seated in their living room; Mrs. Hunt was occupied with some needlework, while her husband was reading a book, probably one he had borrowed from the library. The librarian smiled, thinking it a pleasant scene, until she spotted another figure behind Dr. Hunt.

The librarian knew the Hunts lived alone, so she was surprised to see them neglecting a guest, let alone such a beautiful, well-dressed one. She wondered what was going on when a group of children approached to return books.

"Hello Miss Wardwell," one little girl said. "What are you looking at?"

"Look over there and you can see too," she replied.

Squinting to see through the window, another child quickly piped up, "It's the Hunts and a pretty lady."

"A pretty lady? Are you sure?" Miss Wardwell asked.

"Why of course! She's got a white dress on and she's standing near Dr. Hunt. But he's ignoring her. Isn't it impolite to ignore visitors, Miss Wardwell?"

Now convinced that she wasn't seeing things, the librarian said simply, "Yes, it is, my dear. It most certainly is."

The next day, Dr. Hunt stopped by the library to borrow a Walter Scott novel. Miss Wardwell, like Nelson, was somewhat embarrassed about her interest in the stranger, but asked after her anyway. "Sorry to pry, Dr. Hunt, but who was your visitor last night? I didn't recognize her, and I rather pride myself on knowing who's who."

"Visitor? Hmm. Louise and I were alone," he replied, furrowing his brow.

The librarian described the woman she and the children had seen through the window.

Reluctantly, but diplomatically, Dr. Hunt revealed his secret. "You must have seen Sylvia. You see, she's our ghost; Louise named her. I know that must sound preposterous, but it's true. Ever since we moved in, we've seen her on a regular basis. We have no inkling of who she is. We can't communicate with her, so her identity remains a mystery."

So who is Sylvia? We probably will never know. Some people suspect that she was a guest of the original owners, who lived in the house during the Civil War. It is thought that she became so distraught after learning of her fiancé's death in the war that she threw herself off a balcony onto the brick walkway below. Her grief made her a ghostly prisoner at Panola Hall.

This explanation appears to make sense, but it doesn't resolve the issue of Sylvia's snobbery. The ghost earned a reputation for superiority because she would only appear before people such as the Hunts, who occupied a class similar to her own. If she were indeed a distraught spirit, why would she be so choosy?

Sylvia's last recorded appearance took place in 1929. Mrs. Hunt lay dying, and relatives were set to arrive to pay their final respects. Dr. Hunt, the nurse and the cook were all downstairs tending to Mrs. Hunt. Bessie Butler, a friend of the family, had come to help out. As she looked out the window of a guestroom, she heard someone walking gently behind her. A feminine voice beckoned, "Miss Bessie. Oh, Miss Bessie."

Bessie turned around and noticed a white blur in the corner of the room beckoning her. Terrified, she dashed out of the room and downstairs. She frantically explained to Dr. Hunt that Sylvia had appeared before her. Dr. Hunt ordered everyone to be quiet as he gingerly approached the staircase, but he heard nothing. "She must be gone by now. If you'd stayed up there, Bessie, you might have received a message from her."

Why did Sylvia appear for Bessie that day? It might have been a dark omen, since Mrs. Hunt passed away the same day. Was Sylvia trying to tell someone of Louise's impending death? Or was she simply being mischievous?

We will probably never know, since sightings of Sylvia ended after Dr. Hunt moved out. In 1946 Panola Hall was sold, and today it remains one of the finest historic homes in the quiet town of Eatonton.

4
Strange Stories and Legends

Cogdell Light
Near Waycross

Like many couples from the town of Waycross in southeast Georgia, Ed Jordan and his girlfriend, Cathleen Dupree, liked to drive along the fringes of Okefenokee Swamp in search of the perfect make-out spot. One night in August 1999 seemed like any other, until they had an unforgettable encounter that changed their lives forever—and for reasons that no one could ever have imagined.

The couple had been dating for eight months. Ed, an unemployed motorcycle mechanic who claimed that his blood was "50% swamp water," had enjoyed the thick air and the sounds of egrets and pig frogs since childhood. He brought his girlfriends to a spot he called the Sloop, at the end of an old dirt road, right on the northeastern edge of Okefenokee National Wildlife Refuge. Home to countless species of flora and fauna, with a handful of interpretative centers and scores of cypress boardwalks, the swamp covers some 700 square miles and attracts visitors from across the South.

For his part, Ed found the place as romantic as others might find an expensive restaurant or a long walk on the beach. "I never could figure why the romance ads in the paper never said 'I like romantic nights beside the swamp,'" he says. "I loved it there!"

For years, stories had been told of mysterious happenings in and around the swamp, some connected to Indian tribes from hundreds of years ago, others of more recent vintage. Ed's friends, being born storytellers, told fantastic yarns involving strange lights, headless swamp things and people who ventured into the swamp, never to return. Ed enjoyed the stories, but he considered them little more than fishing-boat folklore.

Cathy came from another world. The Augusta native fancied herself a city girl and looked down on the swamp; it was soggy and hot and filled with katydids, crocodiles and other disgusting things. Her fear of water, connected to a near-drowning incident when she was in kindergarten, was another issue. She suffered Ed his swamp fixation, but only because it afforded them a chance to be alone. Soon enough, however, she planned to use one of their parking sessions to end the relationship.

"I wanted to break up with him," says Cathy over the phone from Hinesville, where she now lives. "He was like a little boy. All he wanted to do was go to the swamp and ride his ATV. He hated to talk about our relationship because he didn't have any idea what to say. For more than a month I had expected him to ask for my hand in marriage. Then I gave up and decided to move on. I thought a break up in the swamp would teach him a lesson."

The couple arrived at the Sloop around 9:30 PM. The light was failing as the sun made its descent, leaving a brilliant magenta sky in its wake. Ed switched off the car and flashed the headlights two or three times. According to local lore, this gesture was said to summon the ghosts that haunted the area. Ed had repeated the action countless times in Cathy's presence, and the ghosts had never appeared; he had always hoped this would calm her jumpy nerves. According to Cathy, he had always secretly wished for something weird to happen. Tonight he would get his wish.

Ed and Cathy remember exactly what they talked about that night, because subsequent events burned the conversation into their memories.

"I wanted Ed to be calm when I told him it was over," Cathy said. "Looking back, I realize how stupid my plan was, you know? He gets upset easy, and he could have left me there alone in a huff—deep in the pitch dark swamp, with all those millipedes and lizards. I should have told him at the house. But it turns out that everything happened for a reason—and I mean everything."

After Cathy broke the news, Ed got upset. The pair fought for nearly an hour as Ed complained about Cathy's high expectations, and Cathy wondered why he didn't want to find a better job and take the next step in life—namely, marriage. The time flew, and before either of them realized it, it was pitch black outside. They sat in the car with nothing left to say.

Meanwhile, utterly unbeknownst to the splintering couple, Todd McIntyre and two of his friends were about to play the prank of their lives. The 16-year-olds were aspiring juvenile offenders who loved to huff solvents and set mini fires around the swamp. Over the past three weeks, they had skipped school and stolen money from their folks to plan and secure supplies for a "monster big prank." Tonight was the night, and Ed and Cathy had randomly become the targets.

The plan had several different parts, but it grew out of a pyro trick intended to replicate the so-called Cogdell Light, a mysterious, recurring green luminescence ensconced in Okefenokee lore as having paranormal origins.

For his own version, Todd stole flares from his stepfather's sailboat. He placed five of them in an inverted traffic pylon lined with aluminum foil, and covered the base with a transparent vapor barrier, the kind used for painting and to keep insulation dry. When he set the flares off, they would flood the pylon with an intense red light. Then Todd would shift the pylon on its tip, illuminating the trees with a bizarre, other-worldly glow. Tonight was the first time Todd planned to shine the light near strangers, with the goal of scaring them half to death.

"It was so cool, like the Bat Signal or something," admits Todd. "It didn't last for too long, but it also didn't require electricity and was very quiet. Basically I made my very own Cogdell Light and I knew it would be real scary."

Todd didn't know Ed and Cathy, but he had seen Ed's Pontiac Sunfire around the swamp, nearly always with a girl in the passenger seat, and so he assumed that whoever drove the car was familiar with the legendary light and would therefore be terrified if he spotted it. "When he flashed his lights after shutting off his ignition, it was a total giveaway," Todd says. "We knew he was a believer. We set up 25 yards away and waited for it to get dark."

The light was part of a three-pronged attack. When it became dark, Todd would shine the light on some nearby trees to arouse curiosity—and fear—in the car's occupants; there was a new moon that night, so the light would be especially eerie in the pitch blackness. Then Jared Moss, the second accomplice, would approach the car. Dressed in an old-fashioned suit pilfered from a high school drama prop department and covered in fake blood, he would scrape his fake plastic fingernails against the passenger door and then

All of a sudden, without warning, they saw a brilliant red light appear and move across the trees in front of them.

show his white face for a moment before fleeing to an agreed-upon rendezvous point. There he would find Todd and a third kid, Andrew, who was responsible for capturing the whole thing on a video camera equipped with a night vision lens. The three would silently make their escape in a rowboat, under the cover of night. Their intimate knowledge of the swamp would ensure that nothing went wrong, and that the plan was carried out in complete silence. "It was perfect," Todd said. "Totally perfect."

Back in the car, Ed and Cathy had found a new topic: how and when to split up their possessions, as they had been living together for three months. All of a sudden, without warning, they saw a brilliant red light appear and move across the trees in front of them.

They hesitated. Was it the infamous Cogdell Light? Neither could tell, but it was eerie all the same, moving with catlike stealth, creeping along the trees like a prison sentry light, somehow aware of their presence. The source was unclear given the thick darkness, but the light was approaching the car and gathering intensity.

Then there were footsteps near the car. The couple's hearts thumped in their chests a mile a minute. Suddenly the red light died, and the footfalls disappeared. The silence, nearly unbearable, was broken by the screeching of fingernails across the exterior of Cathy's car door. She screamed and instinctively thrust herself into Ed's arms.

Ed was terrified too, but the swamp was second nature to him. When a branch moved, he could identify the tree species; he even knew the different sounds of the insects. So when he heard shoes moving in the dirt along the side of the car, something clicked. He knew the thing that appeared in

Cathy's window wasn't a ghost, and it also occurred to him that the Cogdell Light, at least as far as he understood it, was not red, but green. "Stay here, lock the doors," he said to Cathy. "I'll be back."

Ed got out and spotted someone fleeing for the water. He gave chase like a swamp-savvy bloodhound. When he reached the edge of the water, he could make out a boat moving away and heard the sound of anxious whispers. Without hesitating, he jumped into the swamp and overturned the boat. The three boys screamed as they fell in and flailed wildly in the water, which was only a few feet deep. Before Todd and Jared had time to react, Ed grabbed their necks in each of his massive hands and hauled them back onto dry ground. Andrew managed not only to escape, but also to keep the video camera above water.

By this point, Cathy had shone the high beams on the pathetic spectacle. "It was a sight, let me tell you," Cathy recalls. "Ed's courage took my breath away. I'll never forget how he looked, soaking wet in his greasy coveralls and holding those two boys a full foot above the ground, like dead rabbits he'd just shot."

Some rustling in the bushes made Ed aware of a third culprit, so he shouted into the darkness, "Get back here now! I have your buddies here and you won't get in trouble if you cooperate." A couple moments later, Andrew emerged, hands up, and said, "Don't shoot." For reasons unclear to this day, he had come under the impression that Ed was armed and ready to fire.

Andrew waded through the water, frowning, then stepped onto the swamp bank and sized up his cohorts. Jared's makeup, now smudged and runny, made him look even more grotesque, while Todd was utterly incredulous, unable to believe someone had caught him after all his years of impunity. Before any of them could utter a word, Ed launched into them.

"What the hell do you think you're doing here? You scared my girlfriend half to death! You're all headed to see the sheriff!"

Todd's voice quivered as tears ran down his red cheeks. "We…we…just wanted to scare you. We didn't mean no harm or nothing. Please don't call the cops or my folks. You come here a lot, I know…please…you must've been young once."

Ed pursed his lips. The kid did have a point. He must've set off three lifetimes of fireworks in Okefenokee.

"Cathy," he asked, looking back, "what should we do with these kids?" Before responding, Cathy switched the head-lights from high beams to regular; she could see that the light from them was blinding. Then something incredible happened. About 30 feet away, something materialized above the water. It was out of the path of the car's headlights, so it was very difficult to make out, but it was nevertheless quite real, as all of the five eyewitnesses would later admit.

Ed, still in control of the situation, shouted out to whatever it was, asking it to identify itself. Then he turned to the kids and said, "Is that another one of your friends? Well—" He was interrupted by a train's whistle, which pierced the night sky. It was almost unbearably loud and unexpected, since trains had stopped running anywhere near the area 20 years ago. A figure materialized in the distance, looking like an average sized man, but shorter.

Everyone present, except Cathy, was familiar with the ghosts of the swamp, and they immediately thought of the same thing: the headless train victim.

Long ago, a man's head was apparently severed from his body in a freak locomotive accident. According to the legend, his ghost has haunted the swamp ever since, using a headlight to search for his missing head. Many sightings have been recorded over the years, but most people considered them hogwash—that is, until this eerie August night.

"Let's get out of here," Ed said to Cathy, heading back to the car. "Scram," he instructed the three boys. Everybody took off.

Though she didn't realize it at the time, Cathy believes that her actions might have played a part. "I think we upset someone or something with all that racket. Then when I flashed the lights, I think I summoned the ghost."

As with most hauntings, the appearance of the mysterious apparition was never sufficiently explained. Yet evidence of the sighting should have emerged subsequently, at least in theory. For in the minute or so before he was caught, Andrew had hidden the video camera in the crotch of a tree, fearful that it would be confiscated. Showing precocious instincts as a cameraman, he had jigged it to record whatever happened after he surrendered.

The day after the incident, he returned to recover it. Inexplicably, only seconds before the mysterious light appeared, the tape ran out, so no evidence of the ghost was captured. Was it a coincidence? No one on the scene that night thinks so. Cathy believes that the ghost didn't want anyone to record his presence. "I respect the swamp now," she says. "Before, I was afraid of it and thought it was a dump. Now I realize it's a big part of the community, both for the living and the dead."

After the incident, Ed had an awakening of sorts. He and Cathy patched things up, and today they are married and have one son. Ed gave up the swamp, realizing it was a kind of teenage distraction, and went to school to become a park ranger. The couple settled near the Fort Stewart Military Reservation, and Cathy works as a restaurant manager in Hinesville. The three teens, meanwhile, have parted ways, though they still return to the swamp now and then.

Baby Jane
St. Marys Island

When visitors see a ghost at the Orange Hall Welcome Center and House Museum on St. Marys Island, it's usually Baby Jane Pratt's. Clad in a white cotton dress, with flaxen, honey-colored locks, the ethereal seven-year-old is most often seen in her old bedroom on the second floor, though she has also been seen passing visitors on the staircase. Whatever the circumstances, a feeling of melancholy accompanies each sighting, recalling the tragic circumstances under which she perished more than 150 years ago. For one woman, seeing the ghost of Baby Jane was nothing less than a miracle that gave her an entirely new lease on life.

In the early 19th century, St. Marys was a wild place, with few settlers and little civilization. A Presbyterian minister named Reverend Horace Pratt, newly arrived from Connecticut, intended to change all that by bringing the message of Christ to the people of the rugged island.

A year after his arrival, the reverend married a beautiful young woman called Jane Wood. Jane gave birth to four children, two of whom died. Then, in 1829, she herself died after she fell victim to an unknown illness. Reverend Pratt was crushed, but, being possessed of an optimistic nature, he threw himself into his vocation, even founding a church specifically for African-Americans.

In 1834 Pratt married a cousin of his, Isabel Drysdale, who had been a dear friend to his dead wife. The couple moved into Orange Hall, which was built in the early 1800s by Jane's father. An excellent example of the Greek Revival style, it was the most lavish home in the area and eventually, in 1973, it was placed on the National Register of Historic Places.

The Pratts named their first child Jane in honor of the reverend's first wife. She was a beautiful, golden-haired girl who loved to explore and ask questions about the world she lived in. Unfortunately, Jane's curiosity led to her demise. One day she slipped away from home unnoticed to watch a ship of Acadian immigrants, en route to Louisiana, anchor at the local dock. The French-speaking settlers were kind and considerate to Jane, but during their brief stay they unwittingly passed a strain of yellow fever on to her and to others in the community.

Within two weeks, Jane was complaining to her mother of severe pain. Her lips began to bleed and her skin became jaundiced. A doctor was summoned, and he broke the bad news to Mrs. and Reverend Pratt: her illness was serious, in all likelihood fatal. Jane's fever worsened. The night before she died, she passed into unconsciousness. But not even death could crush the sunshine spirit of the resilient little trooper. She died with a smile on her face.

Today, Baby Jane's room—the front bedroom on the house's left side—appears as it was, with dolls, toys and furniture. Visitors are not supposed to enter the room or touch anything, but some have expressed curiosity upon seeing a little girl inside, peering out the window. Over the years, the house's staff have told eyewitnesses that it could only be the ghost of Baby Jane. Many people have spotted her ghost at the window or sitting in one of the miniature chairs in her room. A feeling of melancholy tends to accompany the sightings.

Suzanne, one visitor who saw the ghost, toured the house in 1997 with her husband Phil. The couple, who run a restaurant supply warehouse in Mobile, Alabama, have seen 35 of the 50 states and plan to visit every single one before their retirement.

It was early in the afternoon on a beautiful, calm day when the couple arrived at Orange Hall. They had driven 450 miles over six hours, making only one stop for lunch in Tallahassee, but their tiredness didn't dampen their spirits. As was her habit, Suzanne had done some research on the house in advance. Her familiarity with the story of Reverend Pratt and the couple's Presbyterian roots made the couple excited to experience the house in person.

As Suzanne wandered through the home, she was enchanted by its authentic touches and old creaks, but she also sensed a strange energy. As she reached the top of the stairs, she suddenly felt someone—or something—touch her on the back of the knee. Assuming it was a little child who had become lost, she spun around to see who it was. She saw nothing, but was drawn by an almost magnetic force to look into Baby Jane's meticulously preserved bedroom. The windows were wide open and the curtains danced wildly as the wind blew in. A feeling of melancholy ran through Suzanne, then dissipated.

Overcome with curiosity, Suzanne rushed downstairs and asked a staff member about the room. She learned that the windows in the room were ordinarily kept closed to preserve the artifacts inside from moisture and direct exposure to sunlight. The staff member also told her that a little girl had lived and died there long ago. Suzanne's curiosity grew even more when Phil, who had been smoking a cigarette outside during the sighting, noted how windless the island was. If that was the case, then what could have made the curtains in Baby Jane's room move so energetically?

For the rest of the day, Suzanne thought about the little girl. As a sufferer of endometriosis, a serious condition that rendered her infertile, she understood how precious a young child's life is and how tragic it must have been to have it cut short. However, as a paranormal skeptic, willing to accept as genuine only the miracles described in the Bible, she was convinced that what she saw was an illusion brought on by tiredness and the historical ambience of Orange Hall.

Later that night, at a local hotel, Suzanne was visited by an ethereal presence as she slept. A little girl muttered some words before vanishing. Suzanne could barely make them out, but she believed they sounded like, "Hope. There is hope. Hope." She woke up in a cold sweat and rolled over to look at the alarm clock. It was around 4:30 AM. She was so shaken and distraught that she could not fall asleep again.

Suzanne related the dream and sighting to her husband over breakfast. As she had predicted, Phil had a laugh about the "twincidents," as he called them, then dismissed them as coincidences. Suzanne outwardly concurred, but something led her to believe that there was a deeper significance.

Four months later, long after the couple had returned home, Suzanne discovered she was pregnant. It was a dream come true, the answer to years of prayers, meditation and soul searching. Her doctor, convinced it was almost impossible for her to conceive, was baffled by the pregnancy, but Suzanne remembered the message from her dream.

The pregnancy had several complications. Gabriel was born prematurely, weighing only 2 pounds 2 ounces, and required weeks of care in the ICU. But he survived with no apparent disabilities, and to this day Suzanne remains convinced that he was aided by the strength of Baby Jane's positive outlook. As a tribute, she gave her son the middle name Pratt.

So does Suzanne worry that Gabriel will die at an early age like Baby Jane? No. While she believes that the life stories of melancholy child ghosts are full of tragedy, the spirits of the same children, even in death, can offer hope for the living.

Natalia and the Singing Friars
St. Catharines Island

Natalia lit the burners on her gigantic new barbecue. Costing nearly $3000, plus $200 for delivery, the Fire Goddess 5500 was specially designed for women who loved to barbecue *and* adored luxury. It had a grilling area the size of a soccer field, two warming racks, a flavor box that gave out a rich hickory scent and even interior halogen lights. The pièce de résistance was a low-wattage *mini-fridge* underneath! Never again would Natalia watch fresh iceberg lettuce wilt in the early evening sun over St. Catharines Island.

It did not matter that she knew no one apart from some University of Georgia ornithologists who worked on the other side of the nearly deserted island. The fact was, her barbecue was undeniably cool, and it was just the kind of thing a 42-year-old woman should treat herself to during a messy divorce.

Natalia lived in a small shack along South Newport River on St. Catharines Island. She moved recently from Atlanta hoping to get her head straight before her divorce was finalized. Her department at the university had given her a grant to do some research on endangered turtles, long a passion of hers, so she jumped at the chance; the research and the distance, she hoped, might take her mind off her ex-husband, Stephen.

While she had originally planned to stay for two months, three had already passed. The thick, forested beauty of the island was enchanting, and she spent long hours in her expansive yard, watching the palmettos and listening to the trilling of the cicadas.

Tonight it was muggy and hot. Mosquitoes buzzed constantly in her ear, but they failed to deter Natalia from her long-anticipated barbecue christening. With the chicken and corn cooking away, the only thing missing was music. She ran inside and returned with her old portable stereo. After turning on a cassette, the only one she brought, she stretched out on a chaise lounge and sighed contentedly...

Her mai tai slipped out of her hand onto the grass. She didn't notice. The warm night, the sizzle on the grill and the gentle music had lulled her to sleep.

She was shocked awake by acrid smoke in her nostrils. She leapt up, saw the billowing smoke and turned off the barbecue. The chicken was blackened beyond recognition and all the water had boiled out of the corn pot, leaving superheated cobs of brown mush. The pot was burned through and her calves were covered in throbbing mosquito bites.

Miffed but too groggy to care, Natalia decided to drag herself to bed inside. She flipped the switch on her stereo, but the music still played. She jiggled the on/off button a little, assuming it was a mechanical error, but the music persisted and got even louder.

It was beautiful. A strong male voice, chanting in a foreign language, led a choir that repeated his words in a lower key. The source was unclear, as were the words, but the power was not: the music rose and fell like a powerful tide. After a minute or two, the voices arrived at a striking crescendo, vibrating for an eternity on a single note, then ceased.

Silence. Only the sounds of the wind through the marsh reeds and the trembling oak leaves remained.

Natalia tossed and turned in bed that night, trying to determine the source of the mysterious music. No one lived nearby, so it wasn't the neighbors. The notion, too, that winds through the marshes could have created such deep, powerful rhythms was not convincing either. The chanting had words, beautiful Latin-sounding words, which she found somehow familiar. They gave her a feeling of Zen-like tranquility, of deep peace, but they also unsettled her: beneath the benediction was a deep, inconsolable melancholy.

The sun hurt her eyes the next morning. Had she dreamt up the whole thing in a drunken stupor? Two mai tais and the thick coastal heat could have that effect. But over the next week, she heard the magical chanting again and again. Every night, just as the sun set, she was drawn outside, almost as if under a spell. Each time the voices sounded more and more familiar, and she was soon able to separate them into individuals, although she remained unable to pinpoint their origins. On the fourth night, during a light drizzle, she heard a familiar string of words during one of the chants. She knew them, but from where? She drew a blank.

The next afternoon, Natalia went out on her little aluminum boat. She needed to get some work done. About 75 yards from the shore, while handling a riverbed monitoring device, she noticed a small fishing trawler out of the corner of her eye. It kept getting closer and closer until it was a little less than 20 yards off her bow.

"God bless you, my dear!" the mystery boatman called out when he caught her glance. Having got her attention, he sailed by.

Natalia recognized the voice immediately. It was Father Peter, the former priest at Our Lady of the Seven Holy Wounds Parish back in Atlanta. She hadn't seen him in 15 years, maybe more. His hair had grayed and thinned considerably, but his kindly Irish brogue still boomed unmistakably, even over the splashing of the choppy waters.

She yelled his name again and again to get his attention, but he was pointed in the other direction and didn't hear. Finally Natalia picked up a can of pop and threw it. It struck the back of his boat, right above the name *Carrie-Tas*, and made a loud thump before sinking into the water.

Father Peter turned around, surprised, then nimbly guided his boat back alongside Natalia's.

"Father Peter? Is that you? It's me, Natalia Yakubovich."

"Hmmmm," he muttered, spinning a Rolodex of family names in his head. "Ah yes, Miss Yakubovich! I remember your father Dmitri and your mother—Eva, right?"

"Elena."

"Well come aboard, my dear. It's not every day I meet one of my flock on the river!"

Natalia tied her little boat to his and climbed aboard. After offering her a couple fingers of whiskey, Father Peter explained that he navigated the river to fish and escape the pressures of life in "Hotlanta." She offered her story in return, omitting the bad parts, then asked him a question that had been on her mind.

"Father, I know this sounds pretty weird, but did missionaries ever live on St. Catharines?"

Returning a quizzical look, he said, "Why, yes. Yes they did, Natalia."

He explained. Some 200 years before James Edward Oglethorpe, the legendary founder of Georgia, "discovered" the area in the 1730s, an explorer named Lucas Vasquez de Ayllon set up a mission somewhere near St. Catharines and Sapelo Islands. It failed, and its whereabouts remain unknown, but it set the stage for subsequent missions. In 1565, the Spanish governor of St. Augustine, Pedro Menendez de Aviles, arrived and proceeded to set up 38 missions across the Southeast, with 70 Franciscan missionaries and some 25,000 Indian converts.

Menendez arrived at St. Catharines in 1566 and was welcomed by the chief of the local Indians, Guale. The Spanish soon established a Franciscan mission on the island called Santa Catalina de Guale; it was the northernmost outpost of the Spanish Empire in America in the late 16th century. With patience and determination, the friars converted, educated and inspired the so-called Guale Indians with hopes of a world beyond ours.

Most of the Indians obeyed the Europeans, but some were reluctant to sever ties with their longstanding Indian traditions. In 1597 a Guale called Juanillo led a revolt in which two missionaries on St. Catharines were killed and the mission was set ablaze. Although the Spaniards captured and killed him and rebuilt the mission, a much bigger problem was on the way: the English, who in their southward push were eager to drive out their Spanish colonial rivals at any cost.

In 1680 British forces attacked the mission at St. Catharines. The Indians repelled them but abandoned the mission, as did the Spaniards, ending their involvement on the Georgia coast. The Guale, who had hunted and lived there for thousands of years and about whom very little was known, were gone, never to be heard from again.

Or were they?

"Did the missionaries sing or chant?" Natalia asked breathlessly.

"Indeed they did. They also taught the Indians to sing their antiphonal chants in Latin. According to letters written by the head friar, some of the young braves made excellent singers, their high voices blending beautifully with those of the older missionaries. We sang English versions of them in our choir."

Natalia realized why some of the chants sounded familiar, even after all this time. She had heard them as a child in church.

"Unfortunately," Father Peter continued, "little remains of the Franciscan mission on St. Catharines. Materials used to build shelters have been unearthed, but they date to the Colonial period much later. Over the centuries the mission was probably overtaken by the island's thick vegetation." He paused. "Why, if I may ask, are you so curious about the missionaries? It's almost ancient history."

Natalia suddenly got worried. Father Peter was a bright man, obviously, and she suspected he'd laugh at her stories of ghostly chanting.

"I'm just curious, you know, curious," she said vaguely.

The only way to convince Father Peter about the music would be to invite him home and let him hear the music for himself. She hadn't entertained since she moved in, so the idea seemed grand. Father Peter accepted graciously: clearly he was up for an adventure.

By the time they got back to her place it was 6:00, shortly before dusk. A pink envelope waited in the mailbox, probably a greeting card for her recent birthday. She wanted to open it, but she decided to save it for later. After serving some leftovers, she invited Father Peter outside.

"Nice barbecue," he said, walking past her Fire Goddess. "Beautiful view. Spend a lot of time out here?"

"That's why I invited you here, Father. You see, every night for the last week I've heard music out here at dusk. I couldn't explain it for the life of me, until I heard you talk about the Franciscan friars today. I think they never left! I know it sounds ridiculous, especially for a scientist, but I believe they continue to chant from the marsh over there, mourning the loss of their mission. As a favor to me, would you listen tonight, just for a little while, so I know that what I'm hearing is real?"

Father Peter agreed. She refilled his whiskey, and they waited. And waited. Half an hour passed. Nothing happened. Insects buzzed. A mockingbird cried out. But nary a note rose from the marshes or from anywhere else. Father Peter scratched his head.

"Natalia, my child," he said. "What's *really* the matter? There are no secrets from God. Have you anything to confess—"

"No! The chanting is real, I swear! They're the ghosts of the Franciscan friars!"

She started yelling in the direction of the river, begging the friars to resume their irresistible chorals. Nothing.

Father Peter, growing impatient, downed the rest of his whisky. He'd dealt with a lot of strange people in his day, but he was old now and it was getting late—time to go.

Natalia wandered inside. *Well* that *was a weird little episode.* As she reached down to fix herself another mai tai, she noticed the envelope. She picked it up and tore it open. Although it was fancy and pink, it was no birthday card. It was a wedding notice; in five weeks Stephen would marry again. *What an insensitive jerk!*

Natalia went outside again to reflect on her so-called life. *Let's see.* Her ex was about to move on, probably with a woman he knew while they were still married. Her experiments were a mess. She lived (and occasionally drank) alone in a tiny shack by the river. Finally, most bizarrely, she was unable to convince a whiskey-drinking priest that *ghosts sang every night in her backyard.* Maybe she *was* crazy.

Just then, she heard something. She cocked her head and rolled her eyes, faintly but clearly sensing the chanting of the friars. It began low and uncertain, as if the singers were just gearing up, but the volume rose along with their confidence. Each word became clear to Natalia. She felt as if the singers were finally able to sing more personally, to express all their melancholy to her, now that she knew it was them. They had finally connected.

But how could she prove it to anyone? She looked around and caught sight of her old stereo sitting by the back door. If she recorded the friars, she'd have hard evidence of their existence and prove, once and for all, that she wasn't some middle-aged lunatic.

She hauled the stereo over to the lawn's edge and placed it on the barbecue where the electrical outlet was. The tape in the machine was a copy, so she could record over it and finally get the proof she sought. To test the machine, she rewound the cassette and hit REC and PLAY. The squeaky old gears turned slowly but surely. After 30 seconds, she rewound it and played it back. The resonant sounds of the friars came through loud and clear, drowning out all the other noise. She hit REC and PLAY again as the chanting rose to a grand crescendo.

Assured of her new evidence, Natalia wandered toward the marsh to see if she could see anything. On previous occasions, she worried that her presence might scare off the singers. But now, with nothing to lose, she walked briskly toward the chanting, drawn by its Siren-like power. She realized that the end of the Guale Indian reservation and her own plight were different and yet the same. The friars sang out because they believed someone might listen and care, and Natalia, in spite of her initial skepticism and unhappiness, had become a believer, a kind of convert.

She reached the edge of marsh, not far from the yard. The moon hung full in the indigo sky and the singing enveloped her, yet she could see no sign of anything abnormal. Then she saw a wispy cloud of smoke float over her head and swirl in the moonlight. Was it a reminder of the day when the mission burned to the ground? Or maybe the sweet-smelling smoke from incense that the friars burned as they sang so very long ago? As Natalia invited the smell into her nostrils, she coughed a bit, then gagged. Looking toward the house, she realized that the smoke was coming from her yard. She dashed back.

By the time she returned, the stereo was fully ablaze. She put out the fire with a bucket of water. Although it was too dark to investigate, it was clear that her stereo, along with the cassette, had been utterly destroyed. The next morning she noticed that the electrical outlet, which ran to both the mini-fridge and the stereo, appeared to have overloaded and caught fire. Yet somehow the barbecue escaped any damage.

Natalia couldn't explain the situation. Her friends back home wouldn't believe her, either—about the chanting friars or Father Peter or why she had come to St. Catharines in the first place. The only solace she took was the memory of the soothing music from beyond that had touched her so deeply.

Today, Natalia plays modern recordings of Gregorian chants to her children and her new husband, Mike.

Georgia Stonehenge

ELBERTON

One of the most interesting sights in Nebraska consists of 20 or so vintage American car carcasses, painted gray, turned upright on their bumpers and sunken into the earth in a makeshift circle. Created in 1987 by Jim Reinder on his family farm, despite numerous objections from local authorities, "Carhenge" was created as a tribute to Reinder's father, Herman, and an homage to its Dark Ages predecessor, Stonehenge.

The similarities between the ancient and modern versions are mostly superficial. Stonehenge was arranged by druids of the Dark Ages to chart the phases of the moon and sun, key elements in their Wicca-like religious rituals. Carhenge has no such religious significance. And in place of Stonehenge's enormous quarried stones, laboriously cut and erected by mysterious means, Carhenge's cars arouse little sense of mystery or awe.

So what is the meaning of the structure? On the Great Plains, where the car is king, Carhenge is an unintentional tribute to America's most beloved symbol of convenience, self-determination and, yes, pollution: the automobile. The attraction consists entirely of old cars. The site is accessible only by car. There's a sizable parking lot. Cars and trucks were used in its construction.

Whatever its purpose or meaning, Carhenge is not the only display of its kind. There are more than 10 full-size Stonehenges across the country. Some are accurate replicas, others less so; some have a strong message, while others have no message whatsoever. One under construction near Santa Fe, New Mexico, will consist of old refrigerators and is called Stonefridge. Its creator, Adam Horowitz, says his version will make a statement about consumerism in the United States.

Perhaps the most meaningful American Stonehenge, and easily the most mysterious, is the so-called Georgia Guidestones. There may not be any ghosts involved, but there is paranormal potential. Bankrolled by an unknown group and erected in 1979, the set of six massive granite stones dominates a remote hilltop clearing in Elbert County and remains an interesting, if somewhat controversial, statement about conservation, diversity and peaceful coexistence. Confirming their spiritual power, the guidestones have seen their share of unexplained activity, but there are many objections from groups that want them dismantled.

More than 25 years after its construction, the story behind the guidestones remains a mystery.

On a Friday in June 1976, a man entered the Tate Street offices of the Elberton Granite Finishing Company. The proprietor, Joe H. Fendley, offered to help the gentleman, who was dressed in a suit and carried a briefcase. The man explained that he wanted some oversize pieces of granite cut and engraved. Fendley replied that his company did not vend to individuals. The man smiled and replied that he had come on behalf of an anonymous out-of-state group that wanted to leave a message for future generations. Money would not be an issue.

Fendley offered his hand and asked the man for his name. "Call me R.C. Christian," the man replied, adding that he was a Christian but the project he wanted to propose was strictly non-sectarian.

As they talked, Fendley became more and more interested. The project in question, a kind of latter-day Stonehenge, would represent a lucrative and challenging contract. But Christian seemed a bit apprehensive. After all, the project was no mere gravestone or mausoleum: it would involve enormous slabs of granite, sophisticated transportation and laborious engraving. He needed assurance that Fendley had the necessary resources to carry it off. To this end, Christian was sent to meet with Fendley's banker, Wyatt C. Martin, president of the Granite City Bank.

Christian presented his proposal to the banker, adding that a non-tourist site in Georgia would be ideal. The rich deposits of granite nearby and the mild weather would ensure that the incredibly heavy stones could be quarried and moved without extravagant expense and would not deteriorate over time under harsh weather conditions. Once erected, it was thought, the stones would stand for as long as their famous precedents, such as the Egyptian pyramids, the heads on Easter Island and, of course, Stonehenge.

Martin, like Fendley, listened with great interest, but as a banker he was wary of the secrecy involved. When he tried to confirm Christian's full name and Social Security Number, the man replied that he preferred to operate under a pseudonym.

Martin explained that he'd like to work with him, but it was essential that he provide his real name. When Martin promised that he would do everything to keep Christian's identity secret, during the contract and thereafter, the two men agreed.

Christian left for several months, and Fendley and Martin began to suspect that the whole affair was a practical joke.

But their client was busy making preparations. He returned to Elberton with a precise set of instructions on the construction and engraving of the stones. Since the alignment of the stars figured into the blueprints, meticulous care would be needed to keep measurements as accurate as possible. A large hole drilled into one of the stones was meant to concentrate the sun's light in a meaningful way.

An ideal site was identified in Elbert County atop a treeless hill on the farm of contractor Wayne Mullenix. The five-acre plot was the highest point in the county, an important consideration in the event that aliens or foreign aircraft landed in the future. And at such a safe distance from Atlanta, a potential target in a nuclear attack during the Cold War, it was thought the stones could resist the impact. Finally, the site was near Al-yeh-li A lo-Hee, the center of the universe, according to Cherokee legends, and a deep source of spiritual energy.

Experts were called upon to translate the words into foreign languages, including four "dead" languages: Ancient Greek, Sanskrit, Babylonian Cuneiform and Egyptian Hieroglyphics. The modern languages used were English, Arabic, Hindi, Swahili, Chinese, Russian, Spanish and Hebrew. Examples of the 10 guides are "Maintain humanity under 500,000,000 in perpetual balance with nature" and "Protect people and nations with fair laws and just courts." Another one read, "Avoid petty laws and useless officials." A more detailed explanation follows each of the guides. Their aim was the conservation of the planet and the peaceful, progressive coexistence of all its citizens, with advice on the following universal themes: governance and the establishment of a world government, population and reproduction control, the environment and man's relationship to nature and spirituality. It was vitally important to avoid affiliation with any particular person or group, sectarian or otherwise. Doing so might jeopardize the monument's broad message, which was intended for everyone. Christian expressed hope that other conservation groups would come forward in the future to erect other stones engraved in additional languages, but it has never happened.

There are six stones in total, five upright ones and another—the Gnomon Stone—which hangs suspended over the center of the ring. The upright stones weigh about 40,000 pounds each and stand 19 feet high on top of base stones, each weighing about 4000 pounds. The center stone weighs about 21,000 pounds and is about two feet thick. A hole was cut in the middle of the Gnomen stone as a kind of window that aligns the positions of the rising sun at the summer and winter solstices.

Journeyman sandblaster Charlie Clamp etched the four thousand characters, each three inches high, into the four granite guidestones. The only name that appears on the guidestones is that of R.C. Christian, although a long passage of text places the guides in greater context. One of the key sentences reads, "We hope [our ideas] will hasten in a small degree the coming of the Age of Reason." What is meant by that and some of the guides has been debated since the guidestones were unveiled in March 1980.

Given the variety of possible interpretations for the guides, perhaps it's no surprise that diverse groups, including witches, druids, Native Americans, Christians and Neo-Pagans, have conducted ceremonies at the sight over the years, and not entirely without incident. On September 12, 1980, a round, brightly illuminated object was reported hovering over the monument and in several neighboring counties. A satisfactory explanation has never been given.

So what can we make of the story behind the Georgia Guidestones? With the anonymous backers, strange mix of New Age and Christian principles and unusual happenings, it seems almost too strange to be true. In fact, some believe that it was a ruse pulled off by Martin and Fendley to stimulate interest in the area's granite industry and bring attention to their small town. But according to a report in the *Elberton Star*, the two men passed a lie detector test in which they claimed that R.C. Christian did indeed exist and insisted on anonymity in his business dealings.

Yet even if the whole affair was indeed legitimate, the guides have still had their share of critics. One group calling itself "The Resistance" has even called for the dismantling of the stones. In 2004, its spokesman, John Conner, author of a publication called *The Resistance Manifesto*, claimed that the guides present a Satanic message in the guise of neo-Christian goodwill. "The satanic Georgia Guidestones must be destroyed," he wrote. "The Guidestones should be smashed into a million pieces, and then the rubble used for a legitimate construction purpose."

One can only imagine how R.C. Christian would react. Perhaps the irony of his anonymity, respected to this day, is that he cannot come forward to dispute these claims or label them as ridiculous. In this, he resembles the equally anonymous Druids who built Stonehenge so long ago with a very particular purpose but with no guarantee that anyone would ever truly understand it.

The LaGrange Hound
WRIGHTSVILLE

Randy came back! Or so thought his former owner one night when the dead dog bounded up to the house that had been his home for nearly 13 years. Was it an illusion brought on by incurable nostalgia? Or had the incorrigible old hound, still famous throughout Johnson County for an unprecedented act of heroism, once again summoned a miracle?

Wrightsville is a small community of 2200 people, located 75 miles southwest of Augusta. For the most part, locals keep to themselves. But the community's animals have a tendency to bring people together, even on days when the sweltering Southern heat begins to melt tar patches on Route 319, the town's main artery.

Like most of his neighbors, livestock farmer Jesse LaGrange owns a number of animals.

"My daddy always had critters about," he says, "even before we moved from Kentucky. We can't make a living off hay alone, you know."

Among the many pets Jesse has seen come and go, his favorite was always Randy, a rambunctious black bloodhound with an impressive pedigree who was anything but obedient.

"We got Randy from my cousin to help Jo-Anne recover after her operation," Jesse says, adding that his wife required months of bedrest after a burst spleen in 1983. "But that puppy didn't stay in the house five minutes before he ran outside and flew around like a lightnin' bolt. We couldn't ever whip 'im either 'cause he was just too dang fast. All I thought was cousin Teddy gave me a real lemon."

Although Jesse adored the wild young pup, Jo-Anne and their 15-year-old daughter Tammy considered him more of a nuisance. That changed on July 13, 1987, when Randy's speed and sense saved a little boy's life and changed the family forever.

Tammy, the LaGranges' only child, was home alone that day. As was (and still is) their custom, Jesse and Jo-Anne had driven into town to bowl at their favorite alley. Tammy was smoking a cigarette and flipping through a magazine in the family's modest farmhouse.

"I won't ever forget that day," she says nostalgically from her home outside Atlanta. "It was Waylon Jennings on the cover of *Country and Western Music.*"

All of a sudden, Tammy heard Randy's claws skitter across the linoleum floor at the back of the house. Throwing down the magazine, she jumped up and ran into the kitchen, only in time to see the dog's tail disappear through the worn-out dog door.

Tammy pursed her lips, shook her head and took a drag off her smoke: she was accustomed to the dog's ritual. A pair of mischievous raccoons lived in the grove of trees out back, and Randy had an uncanny ability to sense their clandestine visits to the garbage cans. "Randy's Radar," the family called it. Every time one of the raccoons snapped a twig or dropped a half-eaten biscuit, Randy bounded out the back door in hot pursuit.

But this time something was different. As Tammy pressed her nose against the screen door, she noticed that Randy was not headed for the junk pile. He was racing across the fallow field like a greyhound at full clip. Odder still, he was barking like a rabid beast.

"When I heard him barkin' so loud and headin' for the drink, I knew something was wrong," Tammy recalls. Sure enough, when she looked into the distance, she saw some commotion in the deep pond at the edge of the LaGrange property. Tammy quickly realized it wasn't one of the neighboring Pupkin twins horsing around. Someone was drowning. Not bothering to put her shoes on, she darted out the door.

Tammy ran as fast as she could. About halfway, she stopped to catch her breath; half a mile lay between the house and the pond. As she stooped over and wheezed in the sticky heat, she saw Randy dive into the pond and struggle to pull someone out. Whoever it was seemed unresponsive to his help. Tammy feared the worst.

When she finally arrived, Tammy saw Randy pacing around Jacob Slunder, an eight-year-old with Down's Syndrome who lay motionless in the dirt. Tammy shook him feverishly. No response. Then, remembering something she'd seen on the TV show *Quincy*, she began to push her palms into his chest. About 10 seconds later, Jacob's eyes shot open. According to Tammy, he coughed up what seemed like a couple pints of water. But much to her relief—and Randy's—the terrified boy was alive. Randy's tail wagged like crazy.

Accolades quickly poured in. The whole community celebrated the act of heroism during its annual picnic. After a story ran in the local paper about the rescue, reporters came from as far away as Augusta to interview Tammy. The crowning glory was a pair of special certificates for the rescuers, personally signed by Georgia governor Joe Frank Harris and delivered by one of his aides.

"The messenger was very attractive," Tammy adds with a smile. "It was even better than if Ed McMahon had come to the door with all that money."

Now an EMS driver, Tammy says the experience changed her life forever. "At the time, that dog and me were pretty mixed up. I had dropped out of school and had no employment skills. Randy showed me I could make a positive impact in people's lives, and that's why I became an ambulance driver. I also quit smoking."

Randy also changed after the incident. He seemed suddenly more mature, more like a proper, well-behaved bloodhound. He stopped chasing raccoons. He didn't run around indoors. According to Jesse, he even stopped cutting his mouth on steak bones. The LaGranges' royal treatment probably didn't hurt much.

"You never seen a dog love hot dogs so much!" Jesse says. "We gave him so many after the rescue, he learnt to catch 'em from more 'an five yards away. Funny how he couldn't catch a frisbee to save his life."

As dogs' lives go, Randy's was charmed. But like any pet, his days were numbered. By 1995 Randy began to suffer from nausea and dehydration; soon his hair was coming off in clumps. When he died in December of the same year, the LaGranges dug a modest grave for him near the site where he had rescued the drowning boy.

But Randy's story didn't end there. In fact, the most fantastic chapter had to wait another seven years, when the bloodhound's ghost returned to convey a special message to his old master.

In 2002 Jesse invested all the LaGranges' savings in a herd of alpacas. Jesse explains: "I thought there would be alpaca

Jesse adored the wild young pup.

burgers and Southern fried alpaca and coats filled with alpaca feathers. I was wrong. For one, they were ornery all the time. And when I learnt that nobody wanted the meat or the hides, I slaughtered them in a fit of anger so I wouldn't have to feed them any more." He sighs. "Then Jo-Anne left me."

The next evening, the ghost of Randy mysteriously appeared.

"It was the weirdest thing I ever seen, just like *E.T.*," Jesse says, alluding to the mysterious scene in which Elliot meets his extraterrestrial friend in the family shed. "I was sittin' on the porch, not drunk mind you, when all of a sudden I saw something weird on the edge of the driveway."

The 70-year-old removed his ball cap and squinted; it was dark and his vision wasn't so good. But like any dedicated pet owner, Jesse knew his dog. "It was the ghost o' my old hound come back, sopping wet and carrying something in his mouth."

Jesse walked gingerly toward his beloved old hound. Although Randy's tail began to wag, he seemed slightly reluctant to approach his old master. Jesse was as scared as he was excited. As Randy moved, milky traces of ethereal white light followed him.

"Randy?" Jesse whispered, dumbfounded. "Here, boy."

The dog remained still for a moment, then let out a howl as resonant and beautiful as a church organ. *What on earth?* Jesse thought. Unable to bear the suspense, he jumped down into the dirt in an attempt to trap his old dog. But Randy's ghost had vanished. Jesse got up, undeterred, and searched everywhere for his pooch. When he finally realized that Randy was gone, he threw his hat to the ground and rubbed his face with his hands. In the span of one day, his wife had left him, taking the car with her, and he had just seen a ghost. Perhaps worst of all, the alpaca carcasses, piled up near the shed, were beginning to stink. Jesse was sure the carrion birds would come feasting in no time.

Then, out of the corner of his eye, the haggard old farmer spotted something in the dirt where Randy had appeared—something eerily familiar. He knelt down and grabbed it.

"It was Jo-Anne's lucky rabbit foot. That thing had been lost for years. From then on, I was a believer. The next day I borrowed some money, bought Jo-Anne a necklace and got her back. How Randy knew I will never know, but he saved the day once more."

Since then, everything has gone smoothly for the LaGranges, and Jo-Anne, who never liked Randy in life, has come to appreciate the departed rascal. "Randy used to poop in the chicken feed way back when," she says. "He drove the whole family into a state. But today I love that dead hound even more than my bowlin' ball. That's sayin' a whole lot."

Surrency Poltergeist
SURRENCY

The poltergeist had wrought havoc on the Surrency household for nearly a week. Allan Surrency, fearing that his cut-glass wine decanters were in danger of being smashed, went into his yard in the middle of the night amid great secrecy. Having carefully wrapped the valuable items in burlap, he dug a hole in the ground and buried them. Then he breathed a sigh of relief. The decanters were a gift of the Savannah Hunt Club and easily his most prized possessions.

The next morning, he looked out into the yard through the kitchen window and noticed a broken mess. The decanters had been unearthed and broken into countless shards. He excluded the possibility of a person being responsible because he had told no one about moving the decanters, not even his family, and was careful not to be noticed as he dug the hole. In all likelihood, the poltergeist that had terrorized his family over the last week had struck again.

It had all started in 1872, after Surrency arrived home on the train from Macon to the town named after his family (in southern Georgia close to Jessup). Allan's large house doubled as a hotel and restaurant. When he wasn't busy running the town's general store and sawmill, he was at home with his expanding family.

As the train pulled into the station, Allan was surprised to see a large crowd gathered at the platform. For the most part, Surrency was a quiet place where life was almost idyllic, and the locals liked it that way.

When he got off the train, Tom, the shopkeeper from his store, pulled Allan aside and delivered some rather unbelievable news. "A ghost has overtaken your house!"

"A what?" he replied.

"Some evil force, Allan. I can't say what it is, but it sure is ornery."

Allan was a skeptic when it came to the paranormal, but anything that threatened his family deserved full scrutiny. He rushed through the oak grove back to his house.

His family was waiting outside, and his wife had an incredible tale to tell. "I wanted to come meet you at the station, but I was worried about the house. Pandemonium has broken loose!" She took a deep breath before explaining. "I was sitting in the drawing room, knitting, when my needles and yarn were yanked out of my hands. They spun about in the air, then were thrown against a wall."

Allan had heard enough; he wanted to see for himself. He opened the door and entered, putting down the nails and bolts he had just bought in Macon. He slowly went from room to room, making a careful inspection, trying to notice anything unusual or out of place. A few minutes later he emerged.

"There's nothing to be afraid of," he said to his family outside, now joined by various onlookers. "Come on back in."

Just then, the nails and bolts flew from their resting place on the entryway table and spilled out on the porch.

From that moment on, Allan knew that the force, whatever its nature, was not of this world. It would torment his family for no less than five years. By the end of its terrible run, the poltergeist had shattered every breakable item in the house, moved every piece of furniture not screwed down and left the house in a general state of unpredictability and law-lessness.

Unlike other poltergeists, which tend to focus on children, this one went after everyone with equal vigor. The first time Clementine, an adult daughter, encountered the force, she was returning home for a visit. Just as she climbed the stairs to the house, she was met with a terrifying shower of hot bricks. She was horrified and ran away in fear.

The boys in the family claimed that they were the first to encounter the poltergeist. A minister was visiting the family, and as the boys sat with him in the living room, a log spontaneously jumped out of the fire and began floating around the room. As if this wasn't shocking enough, the fireplace tongs and bellows began to tap and move, almost as if in tune. The minister left the house immediately, and the boys raced upstairs to hide. Meanwhile, the grandfather clock chimed repeatedly, and the windows opened and shut themselves.

In the weeks and months following the initial encounters, the Surrencys were forced to adjust to their grumpy houseguest. Every part of domestic life was affected. When meals were on the stove, it would suddenly go cold for no reason; whenever food was served, the serving dishes were upset or cast against a wall. Eventually the family had to start using tin plates and cups because every last piece of glassware and china had been broken. If Allan sat reading a book, pages would be torn out and would then fly about the room.

The poltergeist was also adept at hiding objects and clothing. One of the Surrencys would notice a sock or undergarment was missing and spend days looking for it; then it would turn up in the most obvious place. Allan once became so impatient that he placed a large amount of clothing in a shed behind the house, hoping the poltergeist would leave it alone out there. When he returned inside, the clothes had reappeared in a bedroom, scattered all over the floor.

Guests were also affected. When one of Allan's sisters visited, he immediately briefed her on the poltergeist and its activities. She listened to what he said, but did not truly believe him. She woke up the next morning and discovered that her shoes had been thrown outside. Assuming it was a prank of some sort, she placed her shoes between her mattresses on the following night. They ended up in almost the same place they had materialized the day before. From then on, she was a believer.

Stories of the Surrency poltergeist quickly spread across Georgia. Trainloads of curiosity seekers (some estimate as many as 30,000) from Macon, Atlanta and elsewhere arrived and toured the house, making note of the broken windows, upset furnishings and airborne objects. (It's worth noting that Allan made no profit from all this traffic.) A few visitors even had the bad fortune to be pelted with small pieces of wood stacked outside the house.

One of the most remarkable stories involved railroad ties. Allan Surrency had helped his town earn the distinction of "Crosstie Capital of the World." He would cut down timber on his property, then convert the logs into crossties at his sawmill.

One day, several years into the poltergeist's stay, a large group of people arrived in town to visit the Surrency house. The train's conductor, a skeptic who had been baffled by load after load of visitors, had grown tired of all the crowds and paranormal nonsense. Once all the passengers had got off and headed for the house, he went to the front of the train to talk with the engineer. The men sat down and started talking about the heat that day when they noticed something unusual outside the window of the train. It was a crosstie floating in mid-air! The men went to the window and watched as the tie turned in the air, then floated outside the passenger cars. Finally it embedded itself two feet into the ground. They were dumbfounded. For months following, tourists shaved off splinters of the tie as souvenirs of the poltergeist's activity.

During the poltergeist's five-year reign, there were welcome periods of calm. But just as the family would assume their normal routines after a period of so much unrest, the poltergeist would return with a vengeance. At his wit's end, Surrency moved the family five miles away to a smaller house. Amazingly, the poltergeist followed them, and the disturbing activity began all over. Then, without reason, the activity stopped altogether in 1877, never to recur again. At last the family had peace.

The Surrency house no longer stands, having been replaced by a pecan orchard. Mr. and Mrs. Surrency lie buried in the Cedar Street Cemetery, enjoying the kind of peace in the afterlife that often escaped them while they lived with a poltergeist.

5
Spirits of Savannah

Olde Pink House

The Olde Pink House on Abercorn Street is the only house in Savannah that predates the Revolutionary War. Built in 1771, it was remodeled in 1779 by James Habersham, Jr., who remains its resident ghost to this day.

Dramatic events have transpired in the house, especially during times of political turmoil. The building once served as the first Planter's Bank in the state. In 1812, after the U.S. ship *Peacock* confiscated $100,000 in gold from a captured British Navy vessel, the money was marched through the streets of Savannah and locked in one of the house's two basement vaults, which today is a wine cellar.

During General Sherman's March to the Sea during the Civil War, the house fell into Yankee hands and was used by General Lewis York to plan battle strategy. Subsequently, the house served as a bookstore, a law office and a tearoom.

But probably the most exciting period in the house's history was during the Revolutionary War. Savannah was loyal to the British, but the Liberty Boys regularly gathered in the Olde Pink House to discuss their plans for a new nation. These men, including Edward Telfair, George Walton and others, had to exercise great caution because the Loyalists were aware of their subversive leanings. They would park their carriages a few blocks away, enter through back doors and pretend to conduct official business. Had they been caught, they could have been charged with treason and executed.

The Habersham brothers—John, Joseph and James— were key players in these meetings. Their father, James, Sr., had been a prominent merchant, politician and planter during the Colonial period and was fiercely loyal to Britain, although he did not always approve of unfair parliamentary strictures in the colonies. Among other honors, the elder Habersham was appointed by the British authorities as the overseer of the Bethesda orphanage in Savannah and established what became one of the most successful plantations in the region. Habersham was greatly respected at the time of his death in 1775, shortly before the outbreak of the war. He died deeply worried about a conflict that could, in his words, pit "father against son, and son against father."

Had James, Sr., lived, this might have been the case. During the war, John became a talented military figure for the patriots, as was his brother Joseph, who managed to pull off a daring and dangerous arrest of Sir James Wright, the Royal Governor of Georgia, in 1776. James, Jr., was more of an organizer. As a merchant who had made his fortune in rice and shipping like his father, he was greatly opposed to the taxes imposed by the British.

James took much of his capital and invested it in the war effort, and also used the Olde Pink House, which he owned, to plan key objectives such as the raid on the king's powder machine in 1775 and the apprehension of Governor Wright. The Liberty Boys were never caught, and many of them went on to become Savannah's most prominent business and political leaders.

Habersham's fortunes, however, declined after the war and he was eventually forced to sell the Olde Pink House. After his death he was buried in the Colonial Cemetery beside his father and brothers, but his spirit seems active to this day in the house he once owned. His appearance is connected to the efforts of Hershel McCallar and Jeffrey Keith, who restored the building and opened it as a restaurant just

The Olde Pink House is the only house in Savannah that predates the Revolutionary War.

in time for its 200th anniversary celebration. The business partners revived many striking elements of the original design, such as the elaborate staircase, authentic heart-of-pine floors and impressive fan light in the entryway. They also erected a locked metal gate through which visitors could see the dining room as it appeared so long ago with authentic period wallpaper, fixtures and antique furnishings.

The dining room has seen much paranormal activity over the years. Even though it is quite secure, staff have discovered lit candles after dark and the furniture moved around with no explanation. Some have even seen people in old-fashioned clothing moving around the room late at night.

Habersham's ghost is said to appear most frequently in an upstairs room. After one eyewitness (who prefers to be called Thomas) had eaten dinner in the restaurant in 2001, he asked about looking around the historic house. Accompanied by a member of the staff, Thomas wandered about, marveling at the remarkable state of the old structure. When the pair got upstairs, the staff member was summoned downstairs to seat a large party. Thomas continued on his tour, although he made sure to be as quiet as possible. He was surprised when he saw a man who "had hair like George Washington" and was dressed in a sophisticated suit from the distant past. Trying to be polite, Thomas said hello to the stranger, who he assumed was part of a historical recreation. When the man failed to respond, Thomas tried again to break the ice by complimenting him on his authentic costume, although he was surprised that a restaurant would outfit its staff in such a way. Again, the man said nothing. Thomas was getting nervous, so he raced down the stairs to find his tour guide, who had been gone for what seemed like a long time. When he reached the foyer, Thomas stopped dead in his tracks. There, on the wall, was an antique portrait of the man he had just seen! It turned out to be James Habersham, Jr.

McCallar said that Habersham's ghost is especially prone to appearing on Sunday afternoons. He believes that the house's history, combined with the high-class renovation, has made it a place where Habersham wants to spend his afterlife, reliving key events that helped 13 British colonies become the United States of America.

Hampton Lillibridge Home

You just never know what will happen when you set out to restore a 200-year-old home. Jim Williams, a well-known Savannah antiques dealer and the model for one of the characters in John Berendt's book *Midnight in the Garden of Good and Evil*, would know. A key player in Savannah's restoration renaissance, Williams has restored more than 30 historic properties.

He bought the Hampton Lillibridge home in 1963 and immediately had the house moved from Bryan Street to its present address on East Julian Street. Something of a restoration purist, Williams tried to get genuine materials that would recreate the original details of the 18th-century building. He had bricks shipped in from houses in other parts of Georgia and found functioning paneled shutters.

In spite of his experience in restoring old buildings, Williams never could have imagined the problems his tradesmen would encounter right after the home had been moved. One day, several terrified brick masons dashed out of the house and onto the street, claiming that unseen persons were moving around and whispering. Williams investigated, and to his dismay he heard footsteps one floor up and the sound of furniture being run against walls. When he went upstairs, he found no one. He convinced the workers to return, assuring them that the sounds had stopped. When the sounds started again the next day, the workers once again abandoned their tools.

The distractions became so serious that Williams summoned the Right Reverend Albert Rhett Stewart, bishop of the Episcopal Diocese of Georgia, to the property on

The Hampton Lillibridge home, before it was restored by Jim Williams.

December 7, 1963. Reverend Stewart performed an exorcism in the living room, asking that the evil spirits leave the place. He then blessed the house, hoping that its otherworldly inhabitants would clear out or face retribution from a higher power.

The measure initially seemed to work: tradesmen returned to the site and worked in peace. But after a few days, the activity began again. One worker, who had just varnished the upper level floors, came down after a long day. As he descended the stairs, he heard someone walking around up where he had been working. "Who's up there?" he asked. He was miffed not only because the varnish was still wet, but also because he had called out several times to check that the area was empty before leaving. But when he got back upstairs, he saw that no one was there, and there were no footprints in the varnish. He never satisfactorily explained what happened, and he was not alone: several workmen had similar stories.

Williams moved into the house in May 1964 over warnings from his tradesmen. One night, he sensed someone in his bedroom while he slept. He assumed it was a burglar and shouted at the intruder, "What do you want?" After he heard no response, Williams got up to chase the intruder, who had fled. Williams heard footsteps race down the stairs, but when he peered down the darkened staircase, he saw no one and no flitting shadows.

A particularly unusual event took place when Williams was away and three guests were staying at the house. One of them heard sounds on a higher floor, so he went up to investigate. When he failed to return, the two others went up to see what had happened. There, laying face down on the floor, was the man who had gone to investigate the sounds. Turning him over, they saw a look of pale horror on his face.

In a shaky voice, he said that he felt as if he had walked into a pool of freezing water, and added that he was on the floor because some mysterious force had been drawing him toward an unfinished chimney shaft with a 30-foot drop.

So what can explain the mysterious activity? History offers few clues. The home's namesake, Hampton Lillibridge, came to Savannah from Rhode Island in the late 18th century to run a plantation on Sea Island. His fondness for New England was reflected in his weekend home, completed in 1796, which looks very unlike the other historic properties in town. In place of the traditional plantation architecture, Lillibridge insisted on typical Northeastern flourishes such as a gambrel roof (the only one in the area) and a widow's walk.

After Lillibridge died, his widow married a man who sold the house to another New England planter. Subsequent owners followed. Mysteriously, the great fire of 1820, which consumed more than 450 homes in just over three days, spared the house.

Given the comparative lack of human drama, it's hard to pinpoint the cause of all the haunting activity, although some suspect that the home's relocation and restoration are to blame. They argue that the materials used in the work might have been tainted with negative paranormal energy.

It's also possible that the home's new plot was haunted. Williams told Margaret Wayt DeBolt, the author of *Savannah Spectres*, that a crypt had been uncovered during the excavation of the home's new foundation. Because it was empty apart for some water, Williams thought nothing of it and had the workers cover it over. Is it possible that the crypt, made of materials from colonial times, was somehow connected to the haunting?

Workmen often heard footsteps on the top floor while working.

A final, and perhaps likely, explanation would involve some tragic event from the home's past, such as the apparent suicide of a sailor long ago.

This conclusion gathers support from Dr. William Roll, an investigator from the American Psychical Research Foundation, who visited the house in the 1960s. He concluded that "emotional waves" left over by some traumatic event caused the house to be haunted, although he was unable to offer specifics.

Whatever the cause of the paranormal activity, the Hampton Lillibridge home remains one Savannah's most notorious haunted houses.

The Pirates' House

General Oglethorpe and a small group of colonists founded Savannah in 1733. As the city developed, a 10-acre site on the eastern boundary of the city was selected on which to develop an experimental garden, modeled after London's exquisite Chelsea Botanical Garden.

Called the Trustees Garden, it was bounded to the north by the Savannah River, to the south by Broughton Street and to the west by what is now East Broad Street. The project was the first such garden in the 13 colonies. Exotic flora from every corner of the earth, such as fruit trees, indigo, hemp, spices, grapes and mulberry trees, were planted for cultivation. Many of the species failed to thrive. For instance, the mulberry trees, invaluable for the production of silk, withered in the occasionally rough weather and poor soil, as did the grapes intended for wine-making. But other species, especially the upland cotton and peach trees, grew abundantly and later bolstered the area's burgeoning agricultural economy.

The so-called Herb House dates back to 1734 and adjoins the present-day Pirates' House Restaurant. It once housed the local gardener and is thought to be the oldest building in Georgia. The first governor of the colony, John Reynolds, later transformed the area into a residential garden.

Today, the area where the garden once stood is one of Savannah's most appealing historic neighborhoods, with many businesses and residences situated near the river. It was not always so. In the 18th century, old Fort Wayne stood behind the house. Built in 1759 and named after the war hero "Mad" Anthony Wayne, it was intended to protect the city from attack. It was captured by the British during the Revolutionary War, occupied for a time and later abandoned. As it deteriorated, the area around it became a hot spot for dueling, and it was populated with poor immigrants and listless seamen.

The Pirates' House tavern was built on a bluff overlooking the river in 1752. Set in the Low Country style, it was a rustic, wooden, two-story frame house, unpainted, with a brick basement and wooden shutters painted blue to ward off evil spirits. It quickly became a popular meeting place for seafarers and ne'er-do-wells of all stripes. One Savannah citizen at the time complained that French privateers regularly caroused in the harbor area, armed with cutlasses and daggers and making no end of trouble for the locals. Records show that the piratical brothers Jean and Pierre Lafitte, allies of General Andrew Jackson in the Battle of New Orleans in 1815, called at Charleston and Savannah in the early 19th century.

"Black Dog" and "Billy Bones" were among the notorious pirates who drank their grog in the dark tavern. Captain William Flint, made famous in Robert Louis Stevenson's book *Treasure Island*, is said to have died there one night while shouting at his most loyal mate, "Darby M'Graw! Fetch aft the rum!" Stevenson, who mentions Savannah many times in his classic tale, describes the pirate as "the thirstiest buccaneer that ever sailed."

During its heyday, many sailors quarreled or were killed on the rickety old floors of the Pirates' House. Some unsuspecting young men, unconscious after being heavily plied with drink, were shanghaied along a secret tunnel from the old rum cellar beneath the Captain's Room to pirate vessels waiting on the river. By the time the abductees awoke, it was too late: they were on a voyage across the high seas, with no good purpose in mind. Their treatment on board the pirate ships was little better than slavery.

Eventually the Pirates' House came under the ownership of the Savannah Gas Company. By then it had been recognized by the American Museum Society as a house museum. With great industry, Mrs. Hansell Hillyer, the wife of the gas company president, transformed the old tavern into an exquisite restaurant consisting of 15 separate dining rooms, each of which conjures a unique vision of the past. Today, the cuisine served at the Pirates' House Restaurant is some of the best in Savannah, and tourists and locals make it a popular hot spot, overseen by the ghost of Captain Flint.

One spooky story involved a Savannah resident who wandered into the tavern one day looking for the legendary tunnel. He asked if he could look around the basement. The waiter, who was very busy, agreed: he was used to tourists who wanted to look around the place.

The man entered the basement. Under some old barrels he found what looked like a hole covered over with boards. Since no one was around, the man kicked the flimsy old boards, breaking them, then lowered himself into what he thought was the tunnel. As he shone his flashlight around the space, he saw it was a damp sub-basement, with ceilings no more than four feet high. *Hmmph*, he thought to himself. *So much for the pirates and their escape tunnel.*

Just then he heard a sound, like a small critter scurrying on the dark ground. Most people would be terrified at such a sound, but this interloper liked things that moved in the dark and showed no fear when he encountered them.

Shining his flashlight on the damp floor, he spotted a small cat, which scurried off into a corner and disappeared. The man followed, wondering where the creature could have gone in the sealed basement. Then he noticed a small hole in the wall under which the cat had darted.

The man got on his knees and reached his arm through the hole. The air on the other side was cold and he could faintly smell the river. Using a small army spade he had brought along, he dug a hole big enough to crawl through. He found himself in a musty, pitch-black tunnel, motionless and soundless. The cat he had pursued had apparently disappeared and the man felt much more apprehensive.

He walked forward with his flashlight until he reached a giant mound of dirt right in the middle of the tunnel. After pushing and digging for several minutes, he realized that there was no way through or around it. Figuring his adventure was at an end, he turned back in the direction he came, hoping he could find his way out. Suddenly he heard voices—not like the voices in the restaurant, which mixed with the clinking of cutlery on plates and bouts of laughing, but secretive whispers of men speaking in a foreign accent. He thought it might be British or Irish, but he couldn't tell: all he knew was that the voices seemed to originate on the other side of the tunnel, and they were approaching fast. The man, ordinarily the picture of courage, became deathly afraid—so much so that he froze in fear.

A couple of moments later, the voices ceased. Then, to his astonishment, they became very loud, as if they had just passed through the mound and were right beside him! The man, having turned off his flashlight, closed his eyes and stood motionless. Did the voices sense his presence? Were they aware of him?

After a few silent, tense moments, he heard the faint shuffling of footsteps. With his eyes closed, he heard the sound of heavy boots stepping gingerly along and sharpened metal against thick cotton. Then the voices resumed and headed away from him toward the restaurant sub-basement. As they disappeared through the hole he had crawled through, the man heard a horrible cackling, as evil as any witch's, echoing creepily through the tunnel and beyond. To this day, the man remains convinced that he encountered two pirate ghosts of the historic old house—and he readily admits that he's less confident in the dark.

Mary Telfair

An attractive house on Barnard Street in Savannah was designed by English architect William Jay, and remains a magnificent example of the neoclassical Regency style. The house was built by Edward Telfair, a courageous patriot and one-time governor of Georgia, for his son Alexander in 1819. The art museum that occupies the house today stands as a fitting testament to the influential Telfair family, but appears to owe the most to Mary Telfair, the last person to occupy the home as well as its resident ghost.

Mary and her sister Margaret met William Brown Hodgson during a visit to Paris. Both fell in love with the scholar and diplomat. Margaret was the prettier of the two, not to mention a more interesting conversationalist, and she and Hodgson were soon married on the condition that he relocate to Savannah. He agreed, and the three moved into the Telfair mansion.

Mary never married but developed a strong interest in the arts. The Telfairs occupied the house until her death in 1875, when she bequeathed the house, along with the furnishings and a modest collection of decorative and fine art pieces, to the Georgia Historical Society, stipulating that it be used as an "academy of arts and sciences." It was opened in 1886.

Today, the building is known as the Telfair Museum of Art. It includes two affiliated institutions, the Owens-Thomas House (also a National Historic Landmark building) and the Jepson Center for the Arts, a 64,000-square-foot, multipurpose structure designed by the internationally renowned architect Moshe Safde. The museum owns 4500 works of art, including some striking pieces by American

Telfair Museum of Art

impressionists Childe Hassam and Frederick Carl Frieseke. Decorative items from the Telfair family collection are on display in the lavish Octagon and Dining Rooms, which have been lovingly restored to their original splendor.

As the founder of the South's oldest art museum, Mary became a key early advocate of the arts in 19th-century Georgia. But according to some, she also makes her presence felt as a ghost.

Over the years, staff have noticed unusual things whenever a giant oil painting of Mary is moved. In the mid-1980s, for instance, immediately after the picture was relocated from its customary position in the dining room, part of the ceiling over the spot collapsed, damaging some other paintings. Apparently Mary did not approve of the move.

This activity seems in keeping with her conservative personality. In her will, after all, Mary specified that there be "no eating, drinking, smoking or amusements of any kind" in her museum. Over the years, of course, these prohibitions were slackened with the changing times—although, again, Mary seemed to notice and make herself known.

One of the building's caretakers, who recounted this story only after finding another job, picked up the habit of drinking during his shifts. Not to excess, mind you, but just enough to offset the boredom of sweeping floors and ensuring, night after night, that all the doors in the museum were locked. Soon he had built up a small collection of liquor bottles in one of the closets at the back of the museum. When he knew no one was looking, he would enter the closet, mix a drink, drink it and then return to work. Since he saw almost no one during a typical shift, he worried less and less about being caught.

One night, after he had washed the floors and checked all the doors, he decided to reward himself with a shot of brandy. When he arrived at his closet, he discovered that all his bottles were gone. He rummaged around the closet for almost 20 minutes looking for his stash. While it was possible that some other staff member had discovered the bottles and thrown them out, the caretaker, who was in charge of all the building's keys, had the only copy of the key to this particular closet, which held nothing but cleaning supplies and mops. In addition, he kept the keys on his person at all times. Lacking any other explanation, he became convinced that Mary's ghost was to blame, especially after he walked by her

Mary Telfair continues to oversee the family art collection in the house—even from the afterlife.

portrait and noticed a strange, almost unnatural light shining on it from outside.

To make things worse, the caretaker slipped on a slick floor as he was leaving the building, bruising his thigh. He was baffled because he had washed the floor hours before. How could the patch not have dried? He maintains that Mary had intervened—and for the best. Today, the caretaker would not dream of drinking at his new position.

The mysterious activity is not limited to Mary. Staff have heard harp music echoing through the vacant parlor, and phantom footfalls have also been reported, along with incidents of doors opening and closing of their own accord. The disturbances have left staff baffled, especially when the burglar alarm is set off late at night for no apparent reason. Although Mary cannot be linked to everything, her philanthropy and vision are apparent in every corner of the Telfair Art Museum, even when her ghost is not.

John Wesley

Many people are struck by the statue of John Wesley in Reynolds Square in Savannah. As the founder of Methodism and the author of some 400 books, Wesley's fame is well known, but his relationship with Savannah was a matter of great controversy. After falling in love with a young local woman, the evangelist left the city in 1737 under a cloud of suspicion and disapproval. He did not leave his spirit behind in the city or return as a ghost, but he did have many spiritual experiences himself. Wesley's life was not what one might imagine for such a great religious leader, especially when it came to the paranormal.

Wesley was born on June 17, 1703, the 15th of 19 children to Reverend Samuel Wesley of Lincolnshire and his wife Susanna. John's father was an Anglican rector, and his mother gave all her children a pious education at home.

Wesley suspected his divine vocation from childhood. In 1709 the family home caught on fire. Young John was asleep in his bedroom in the attic at the time and was unable to escape when the staircase was consumed in flames. Wesley's father fell to his knees and prayed for his son's soul, expecting the lad would die. Others gathered outside the inferno were equally distraught.

Everyone except for the child himself. He lifted himself up to the window and crawled onto the ledge. Then he carefully lowered himself into the hands of a man who stood on another man's shoulders. John later claimed, as did his family, that he had been saved by God so he could carry forth word of the Anglican faith.

John Wesley

Wesley's interest in the paranormal can be traced back to a poltergeist that manifested itself in the family rectory when John was 13. According to letters and journals of various family members, the force first made itself known in 1716 and stayed until the following March.

Loud knockings occurred, and family members could hear mysterious groaning noises. Chains would rattle and glass would brake, always with no explanation.

According to her biographer, Susanna, John's mother, saw the poltergeist only once. It appeared under a bed in the form of a headless badger; a servant reported a similar sighting. Susanna became increasingly annoyed with the disturbances. With so many children to take care of, she needed order in her home, and the poltergeist promised only chaos. Yet although he was an annoyance to Susanna, he seemed to respect her desire for silence while she said her devotionals each morning.

Her husband Samuel never saw the poltergeist. He once considered threatening it with a pistol if he ever saw it, but was urged not to by another minister. The poltergeist seemed to take particular pleasure in annoying Samuel while he was in his study.

The children, meanwhile, grew quite accustomed to the force. Although initially terrified (back then, evil forces had terrifying religious associations with the Devil and other dark forces), they soon began to taunt it and to laugh at its attempts at scaring them. John's sister Emilia, who celebrated the poltergeist's presence as an opportunity to convince "myself of the existence of some beings beside the ones we see," nicknamed the troublemaker "Old Jeffrey." Another of the children, Kezzy, considered the poltergeist her favorite playmate. She raced from room to room, imitating Jeffrey's rappings on the walls with some of her own.

It seems that Old Jeffrey left in 1717, but like many poltergeists, he wasn't gone for good. A recurrence was reported in the rectory almost 100 years later. It got so bad that the family occupying the house moved away to London.

What can explain the Wesley poltergeist? A common explanation for such "noisy spirits"—namely, that they are attracted to high concentrations of adolescent angst—seems to fit the situation at the Wesley home, where upwards of 10 teenagers lived. Explanations at the time, however, were more religious or even political. One friend of the family thought that Jeffrey opposed King George because he would raise a great racket whenever Samuel prayed for the goodwill of the king and his family.

Whatever the case, the experience made a lasting impression on John Wesley, revealing the existence of non-divine forces in a world beyond our own. When he was 17, Wesley began to study at Christ Church, Oxford. An extremely diligent student, he oversaw a number of study clubs that met at certain times to read and discuss the scriptures. Among other things, these groups practiced exorcisms and discussed the occult. Other students at Christ Church considered the clubs overly pious and methodical and mockingly labeled their members "Methodists," a label that would assume a very different meaning in time.

Upon graduating, Wesley was ordained as an Anglican priest. He had shown an energetic interest in missionary work, so he decided to move to Savannah in 1735 with plans to aggressively convert the locals and Indians to Anglicanism. They, however, grew to dislike the bible-thumping minister and his regimented ways, and he quickly became one of the most loathed men in town. One congregant became so offended by his proselytizing that she threatened Wesley at gunpoint.

Having failed in his missionary vocation, Wesley took a job as the secretary to Savannah's legendary founder, James Oglethorpe. In his new capacity, Wesley met the city's chief magistrate, Thomas Causton, and his 18-year-old niece, Sophia Hopkey.

John Wesley visited St. Simons and worked to establish a church on the site of the present-day Christ Church.

Wesley was soon hired to teach French to the tall and spirited young girl with hazel eyes and light brown hair. The minister, a rather short man at 5'4" with uninteresting, sharp British features, was hopelessly in love, and a brief and controversial affair ensued.

Oddly enough, Sophia's parents considered the couple a good match and offered their blessing. Causton, her uncle, told him quite frankly, "I give her to you. Do what you will with her. Take her into your own hand. Promise her what you will. I will make it good."

It was Wesley who hesitated. He felt compelled to consider the advice of leaders from another Protestant group, the Moravians, who counseled him against marriage. He also had his own family background to consider. Although he respected his father's status as a minister, he knew that he and his 18 siblings had drawn his father away from his spiritual calling.

Divided, Wesley spent months trying to decide which was greater: his love for Sophia or his love for God. In the end, he decided not to marry her.

When Sophia ran away to South Carolina to marry another man, Wesley was crushed. Later the couple returned to Savannah and attended a mass conducted by Wesley. The minister refused to serve Sophia communion, a very serious offence at the time. A complaint was filed the next morning and Wesley was eventually brought up on public defamation charges. The event became much talked about in Savannah society, with each party (and in particular Causton) offering its own version of the communion refusal. Some said it was revenge on Wesley's part for losing a woman he deeply loved; others believed that there were legitimate ecclesiastical grounds for Wesley's refusal.

Causton, who was outraged at Wesley's behavior, had conveniently stacked the jury at the trial, which began in July 1737. Although a mistrial was eventually declared, Wesley had already been convicted in the court of public opinion. Feeling the pressure from all sides, he fled the city on December 22, 1737.

Although his missionary work was widely considered a failure, Wesley's accomplishments in Savannah were impressive. He founded the city's first Sunday school and he also composed the first hymnal ever used in Georgia. Most important, he set the groundwork for Anglican and Methodist work in the area, which continues to this day at a number of local churches.

Wesley married at the age of 45, but after a year or so, he and his wife moved into separate quarters. She died shortly thereafter, and he never remarried. By the time he died in 1791, Wesley's reputation was remarkable. He published hundreds of books, including grammar for a variety of languages and devotionals and treatises on such subjects as theology, logic and medicine. He traveled hundreds of thousands of miles on horseback as a so-called circuit rider, spreading his new faith, Methodism, which remains one of Protestantism's largest sects.

Even to the end, Wesley retained his interest in the paranormal. One anecdote illustrates this rather well.

In 1772 Wesley received a letter from Emanuel Swedenborg, the famous theologian and precursor to Spiritualism. After a communication with the world of the spirits, Swedenborg wrote, he received instructions to contact Wesley. He hoped they could soon meet, so Swedenborg provided an address in England where he could be reached. Wesley had followed the Swedish seer's career with great interest, but he was away conducting one of his "open air ministries." Wesley replied that he would be happy to visit at a later date. Swedenborg responded that it would be too late by then because he knew, deep in his heart, that he would die on the 29th day of the month. The prophecy, remarkably enough, came true.

Ghosts at the 17Hundred90

The complex of buildings called the 17Hundred90 Inn and Restaurant stands on the corner of East President and Lincoln streets in Savannah. In spite of the name, the Federal-style buildings are not from the colonial period, although they were erected on the foundations of much older buildings dating back to the 1790s.

This sense of the past is further enhanced by the 17Hundred90's interiors. Tasteful antiques and period furnishings fill the restaurant, bar and lounge, complementing the old brick walls, wide beams and flagstone floors. But history is not merely something recreated at the 17Hundred90. According to Chris Jurgensen, former owner of the establishment, the past comes alive in the form of ghosts who inhabit the buildings.

Anna, a spirit from the Colonial period, is the most well-known ghost in the place. Her story is a reminder that not all immigrants who came to America had their dreams fulfilled.

Anna lost her parents in a typhoid epidemic near the British city of Liverpool. With the small inheritance she had received, she decided to sail to America in search of opportunity. She had no profession and was unsure what she would do, but since friends of her family had successfully settled near Savannah, she booked passage aboard a ship.

A week into the long voyage, she met a young woman named Sarah. Sarah came from London, and was clever and ambitious. The two quickly hit it off, spending many hours together aboard the ship playing whist, a popular card game, and sewing garments they would wear in the warm temperatures of Savannah. Sarah intended to make a success of life in America at any cost.

One night, as the two women strolled across the deck of the ship, Anna caught the eye of a handsome young man. Nothing happened, but when the two saw each other again on the following night, the young man introduced himself as William Tucker of Liverpool.

William was a large, powerful man with a booming laugh and a quick way with people. A blacksmith by trade, he had fallen on hard times. His wife had died during childbirth, as had the baby, so he decided to make a fresh start in America. He had no savings to speak of, so finding work was a priority as soon as he arrived.

Anna began to sew a cap that he could wear at his new job in Savannah. The pair spent many nights sitting on the ship's bow talking about life in the 13 Colonies.

By the time the ship landed in Savannah, Anna was certain William would ask for her hand in marriage.

"Let us find accommodations, first," he said.

William found two rooms in a rooming house where the 17Hundred90 stands today—one for himself and one for Sarah and Anna. William and Anna continued to spend a lot of time together, and Anna assumed marriage was in her future. But William put off such a step.

A week passed and little changed. William soon asked to borrow money from Anna to pay for the room, assuring her he would find work very soon. Anna still asked after a proposal, but William created a new excuse each time.

One morning, Anna rose early and left the inn to fetch some breakfast. When she returned, she noticed that William was gone—as was the small purse that carried her money and what little jewelry she owned.

She ran to the room next door and frantically banged on Sarah's door. She, too, was gone. When she looked around the room, Anna noticed some shaving cream in a wash basin in the corner of the room. She also found the wool hat she had sewn for William lying beside the bed.

William never returned, nor did Sarah. Anna searched the city to find them, asking about them wherever she could, but they had vanished. With no money, Anna tried to contact her friends in Savannah. No reply came, and she became more and more desperate.

Work proved extremely hard to find for someone with no skills, and before long Anna began patrolling Savannah's harbor front looking for sailors. With each passing day, her expectations for life in America dwindled, and she began to drink more and more. Five years passed. One spring morning, as Anna wandered the streets, she caught sight of a fancy carriage in front of one of the city's finest boutiques. A woman in an elaborate hoop skirt stepped out. She wore expensive jewelry and an elegant hat that appeared European in its design. Anna squinted to get a better look; something about the woman seemed familiar.

It was Sarah.

Having long ago lost her sense of propriety, Anna rushed up to the carriage and started shouting, "Sarah! I know it's you! You stole my money and I want it back!"

Sarah merely looked away, and seemed not to recognize her old friend. The driver stepped down in front of Anna and yelled for the police. Anna ran away.

Seeing Sarah reminded Anna that five years had passed in what seemed like only moments, and she had nothing to show for it. When Anna looked at her reflection in a nearby shop window, she began to weep. Her body was aged beyond its years, two of her teeth had been broken and her clothes were in filthy tatters.

Anna returned to her rooming house. After drinking nearly half a bottle of gin, she tried to sleep. Nothing worked. By 3 AM, she had had enough. She threw herself off the balcony and plunged to her death on the hard stones of the courtyard below. As she fell, she let out a piercing scream that rent the cool night air.

Even today, guests and staff at the 17Hundred90 continue to hear Anna's bloodcurdling scream, as well as sobs from the room where Anna's room once was. Whether other unexplained phenomena are connected to Anna is unclear. These include the sounds of feminine steps on the stairs, a rocking chair moving with no one in it and windows opening and closing for no reason. In the same room where the sobs are heard, the phone has been known to ring at random. That might not seem unusual, except that all incoming calls to the hotel must pass through the switchboard at the front desk.

One former owner, Diane Greenfield Smith, became convinced of Anna's presence—and of the existence of ghosts in general—in 1982. Smith spent Saturday afternoons alone in the bar going through the restaurant's books. On several occasions during the hot summer that year, she felt incredibly cold air surround her. On one occasion, while she was stocking the kitchen fridge in the back, some unseen person or force pushed her out of the way. She suspected it was Anna because she could hear the sounds of a woman's old-fashioned heels clicking on the floor and her bracelets jangling in the darkness. Smith suspects that Anna's ghost is seeking the attention and recognition that she lacked in life.

Anna is not the only spirit in the 17Hundred90. A young girl from the 1820s is also thought to haunt the building. Her story is not as tragic as Anna's, but no less moving. The little girl, an orphan, showed up on the doorstep of the house one day, hungry and upset. She was soon taken in and cleaned up and became one the house's best young helpers. According to former owner Chris Jurgensen, she came down with consumption and passed away before being able to fulfill her great potential. Her spirit conveys a sense of great solitude and melancholy.

A final spirit is that of a cook who worked in the house in the 1850s. Described as a large woman with an intimidating presence, she doesn't like anyone coming into her kitchen. Her ghost puts off a threatening aura apparent to the other help. But, though she might not like it, the restaurant continues to operate, even thrive, without her and despite her ghost.

6
More
Historical
Haunts

Grove Point Plantation
Near Savannah

The film *Cape Fear* was filmed at Grove Point Plantation south of Savannah in 1962. Robert Mitchum played Max Cady, an unrepentant psychopath obsessed with terrorizing attorney Sam Bowden (Gregory Peck) and his family as payback for a murder conviction years before. Even today, Mitchum's performance remains one of the most frightening in cinema history. And while stories of ghosts at Grove Point may not be as terrifying as J. Lee Thompson's film, they have retained their appeal through the years.

Some stories about Grove Point involve pirates and hidden treasure. It is thought that the infamous pirate known as Blackbeard, aka Edward Teach, used Grove Point as a retreat and even set up a slave compound there in the 1700s.

Blackbeard got his start on a privateer, a ship hired by the government during wartime to attack the enemy and steal their cargo. He showed excellent instincts, pilfering on Queen Anne's behalf from many French and Spanish ships during the War of Spanish Succession. He later apprenticed for another famous pirate and was soon looting ships with impunity all along the Atlantic Coast, from Nova Scotia to the Virgin Islands.

Blackbeard is probably the most famous nonfictional pirate ever, although not in terms of sheer plunder. Part of his success is a result of the image he created. He grew his hair and beard very long, tying colored ribbons in them. He often lit a slow-burning piece of hemp in his hat, which enveloped his head in smoke. Wearing several pistols and carrying a razor-sharp cutlass at all times, he hoped to have others surrender upon seeing him, and it often worked. The irony was that Teach was affable and quick to laugh, not to mention a hopeless romantic.

Eventually, the law caught up with him. Robert Maynard of HMS *Pearl* is credited with tricking the pirate, dueling with him and then shooting him. In keeping with his legendary status, Blackbeard apparently died only after being shot and stabbed multiple times. His head was hanged from the bowsprit of the *Jane*, Maynard's sloop.

Blackbeard's ties to Grove Point are attributable to the daughter of a former resident. She wrote that the overseer of a slave colony on the grounds walked with a limp and lived with a mysterious "white lady" near where the main house is today. As is often the case with stories of famous pirates, rumors of hidden treasure also circulate: it is thought that Blackbeard's was buried somewhere between the house and the river, although no chest has ever been unearthed (nor has Blackbeard's treasure ever been found).

In 1830 John R. Cheves of Charleston bought the property and erected a grand brick house. Modeled after a German castle, it had a room in the tower, steep walls and an unusual façade. Federal troops overran Cheves' land in December 1864 during the Civil War. Cheves, who had been working on an explosive device for the Confederacy, apparently died of a stroke when he realized the enemy was nearby. Attempts to bury the efforts of his labors resulted in a depression still visible in the yard today.

Three Yankee soldiers died near the property and are said to be buried on the grounds. Union troops stayed at the house for months, using it to signal ships on the river.

Before leaving, the soldiers stole all the gold and silver, consumed all the perishables and set the house ablaze.

After the war, Grove Point sat abandoned until Ralph Elliot acquired the plantation in 1882. Four years later he built the current two-story brick house. Subsequent owners include the Mercers, a very prominent Savannah family, and Judge Henry McAlpin.

In 1956 the Great Dane Corporation acquired Grove Point and remodeled it for corporate entertaining. The caretakers of the property, Charles and Margaret Edwards, have told many stories about strange happenings on the historic plantation. In the late 1980s, when renovations were underway on the second floor, ghostly activity seemed to occur in a large upstairs bedroom when fresh paint would not dry on the walls. The confused painters tried heat lamps and fans to dry the surface, but nothing worked: the paint remained as wet as the moment of first application. Then, when Mr. Edwards went upstairs to check on the painters, he found they were gone. They later explained that they were overtaken by a strange fear and fled from the house.

Another time, Mrs. Edwards found a guest already in the dining room when she rose to make breakfast one morning. The gentleman wore a quizzical look, so she asked him if everything was okay. He wondered if there was something unusual about the bedroom he had been given—the same one where all the other paranormal activity had been observed.

He woke up suddenly in the middle of the night and saw a woman standing on the other side of the room. Assuming it was his wife, he told her to turn out the light and come to bed. But as he squinted to get a better look, he realized the woman wasn't his wife. It was a stranger who had long, dark hair and wore a glowing white gown. Before he got the chance to identify her, she seemed to float right through the door. He immediately got out of bed to follow her, but by then she was gone. The man returned to bed but was unable to sleep, causing him to be up very early the next morning—somewhat frustrated.

The Edwardses had many similar experiences. The identity of the woman in white remains a mystery. While it's possible she is connected with the property's pirate lore, it's more likely, given her dress and comportment, that she comes from a more modern era. Whatever the case, she continues to make Grove Point one of the more memorable haunted houses in the Savannah area.

Barnsley Gardens

ADAIRSVILLE

What can be said of the curse at Barnsley Gardens near Adairsville? Is it merely a way of explaining the cycle of tragedies that plagued Godfrey Barnsley and his family? Or does it relate to an otherworldly offence against the Indians who once occupied the land where the house was built? You'll have to decide for yourself.

Godfrey Barnsley was born in 1805 in Derbyshire, England. In 1823 he immigrated to America without any formal education or training. Making his way south, he was hired as a brokerage clerk at a successful cotton-shipping firm in Savannah. He showed superior instincts, and by age 25 he had made a fortune in cotton and was well known in Savannah's high society.

Godfrey wed Julia Henrietta Scarborough, the beautiful daughter of a wealthy Savannah merchant, in 1828. The couple soon set off for Liverpool, England, in part for Godfrey's business and in part to escape Julia's meddling mother, who had been heavily opposed to the union from the start.

Because demand for cotton was very high in England, Godfrey traveled constantly to London and New York from Savannah. After the birth of a daughter, Anna, the family settled in Georgia in 1830. The Barnsleys planned to return to England the same year, but a sudden crash in the cotton market wiped out Godfrey's fortune. He was forced to start anew—a situation that came to characterize his shifting fortunes.

Meanwhile, Julia always seemed to be pregnant, eventually giving birth to seven children. In 1838 she was diagnosed with consumption. At the time, Savannah's coastal air was thought to be unhealthy, and cases of yellow fever and malaria were not uncommon.

By the early 1840s, Godfrey's business was thriving again. With his renewed financial security, he set out to design a lavish home surrounded by lush gardens for his growing family. Fearing for the health of his wife and young children, Godfrey sought land close to the mountains, which was considered to have better air.

During a stagecoach expedition to northwest Georgia, which had recently been opened up to land claims, Godfrey discovered a 4000-acre site in present-day Bartow County. It was a beautiful, rolling piece of land, and Godfrey bought it straight away. Several other prominent citizens from Savannah, including Reverend C.W. Howard and W.H. Styles, also bought land and built homes in the area.

In 1844 the Barnsleys arrived at their 4000-acre plot. It was rugged, but Godfrey had laid out meticulous plans. After setting up his wife and children in a temporary log cabin, he had trees uprooted, fences built and a foundation dug for the house. The intention was not merely to erect a plantation house in the Georgia wilderness, but to create a country estate comparable to stylish equivalents in Europe. In the English style, he would name it Woodlands Manor.

Materials were shipped in from around the world: black and white Italian marble, glossy European tile, handmade English paneling and silver key plates. Some of the lavish conveniences included flush toilets and running hot water, drawn from a copper tank near the chimney. As he walked through the developing construction site, Godfrey imagined exactly where he would place the unique furnishings and art treasures he had collected on his various journeys.

But it was the gardens of Woodlands that truly inspired Godfrey. An avid horticulturalist, he laid out gardens inspired by *A Treatise on the Theory and Practice of Landscape Gardening, Adapted to North America*, a popular book by Andrew Jackson Downing, America's first influential landscape architect. Exotic trees, including California sequoias, Japanese yews and Lebanon cedars, were planted, and many exotic roses and other flora were cultivated. Godfrey even had teams of oxen haul decorative stones from the nearby mountains. So impressive were the gardens that neighbors later began to call the property "Barnsley Gardens" instead of Woodlands Manor. The new handle, after all, better reflected the singular vision of the estate's designer.

But underneath this Englishman's very American dream, something unsettling and potentially disastrous lingered—a curse that some say heaped tragedy on the family and ultimately prevented the completion of Godfrey's Xanadu.

In 1838, after a long legal battle over the Indian Removal Act in the Supreme Court, the U.S. government had secured the power to expel more than 15,000 Cherokee from northern Georgia. Seven thousand soldiers were sent to herd them into makeshift forts, supply them with minimal food and force them to march 1000 miles away from the only home they had ever known. More than 4000 Cherokee died during the arduous journey, which coincided with the disastrous winter of 1838–39. The route became known as the Trail of Tears, although it remains one of America's least-known tragedies.

When Godfrey came across his desired spot, it had only recently been cleared of the Cherokee. According to one of his letters, Godfrey found a Cherokee man still living on the land he planned to buy. He hired the man to help out and allowed him to remain for a while, but he explained that he intended to clear the bluff near the creek and erect a mansion on an almond-shaped plot. The elderly man listened to these words carefully, and explained that the hill and the creek on this land were sacred to his people. They had always respected them, and destroying them might invite the wrath of his Cherokee forebears.

Godfrey scoffed at the warning. He refused to change his plans. The two men parted ways, but not before the Cherokee cursed the ambitious developer.

Everything went according to plan. The only times when the work slowed were when Godfrey went away on business, often for months at a time. Although Julia was kept busy by her growing brood of children, she missed her husband and the genteel parlor culture in Savannah. Woodlands gave her little sense of home. In the summer of 1845 she came down with another lung infection. After becoming too sick to walk or write letters, she returned to Savannah for treatment. But it was too late: she died, followed by her infant son.

Godfrey was devastated. Just as his magnificent home was being erected, the very symbol of his accomplishments and dreams, his life was falling apart. Racked with guilt, he blamed his long absences for Julia's decline and death and vowed never to marry again. Had the curse claimed its first victims?

For a much-needed change of scenery, Godfrey moved his young family to New Orleans and traveled constantly from

Woodlands Manor was built with the finest materials from around the world.

there to Savannah, Liverpool and Mobile, Alabama. Once the worst of his grief had passed, he returned to Woodlands to complete construction of the house as a lasting tribute to Julia.

Grief soon turned into an obsession. He began to see his dead wife in his dreams, and he could also be seen deep in thought near the fountain in his boxwood garden communing with her. She offered him advice on the gardens, and Godfrey passed it along to his tradesmen. If that seemed weird, those around Godfrey understood his bond with Julia and his determination to complete Woodlands.

Construction had nearly finished when the Civil War broke out in 1861. As a result of that upheaval, Woodlands began to decline even before its finishing touches, such as the parquet floors and custom-made stairway, had been added.

Godfrey was too old to serve, but his two youngest sons eagerly enlisted with the Confederate Army. The eldest son was away in Asia at the time collecting art treasures for the house, but he never made it back to America. He died under mysterious circumstances in 1862, apparently killed by Chinese pirates.

Federal troops arrived at Woodlands in May 1864. Colonel Robert G. Earle, a member of the Second Alabama Cavalry, made the warning. Approaching the gardens on horseback, he yelled, "The Yankees are coming! The Yankees are coming!" But the enemy was closer than he imagined. He was shot and killed by a member of the 89th Illinois Volunteers within a stone's throw of Woodlands.

General James B. McPherson, a gentleman officer, led the invading Federal forces. After spending a night at Woodlands, McPherson came to appreciate the beauty of the gardens. He was equally impressed by Godfrey's humane treatment of slaves. Godfrey, moreover, was a British citizen who flew the Union Jack and claimed neutrality in the war, so McPherson wanted to spare Woodlands from the looting and burning that was common during the Atlanta Campaign.

But when Confederate bonds were discovered in Godfrey's safe and it became clear that his sons served in the enemy army, McPherson's men were set free in the house. They destroyed statues and ransacked much of the house in search of hidden caches of gold, but found only Godfrey's prized books, furnishings and trinkets. In the cellar they finally discovered something worth carting away: Godfrey's impressive collection of fine liqueurs and wines. Everything portable was either consumed or loaded into supply wagons, and the house was left in a shambles.

When Godfrey saw what had become of his dream home, he sat down and wept. What had he ever done to deserve so much suffering? He buried Colonel Earle in the garden, near where the poor man had been shot, and marked his grave with a stone. Later, when the brave soldier's relatives were alerted to his death, they intended to come and move his remains to Alabama, but word of the Cherokee curse scared them off.

By the end of the war, Godfrey's life lay in ruins. His sons, who refused to pledge allegiance to the new Union, moved to Sao Paulo, Brazil, where their descendents live to this day. Godfrey had invested heavily in Confederate war bonds, which were now worthless, and the once-lucrative cotton trade, the source of Godfrey's wealth, would never be the same.

He had no choice but to try again to pull himself up by his bootstraps. He moved to New Orleans in 1871 in a final attempt to resuscitate his shipping business. It failed, and he died in poverty in 1873. His body was returned to Woodlands, where he was buried next to his wife Julia. According to some sources, a final insult came when hood-lums unearthed his body and cut off his right hand for use in a mysterious voodoo ritual.

Meanwhile, Godfrey's daughter, also named Julia, and her husband, James Baltzelle, a former army officer, and their daughter Adelaide had taken up residence in the house. Like many Southern properties after the war, Barnsley Gardens slipped slowly and inevitably into decay. Weeds overtook the gardens, and the once-shimmering fountain filled with branches and dead leaves. James tried to support his family by selling felled timber from the property. He was struck and killed by a falling tree in 1868, perhaps another victim of the Cherokee curse.

Julia later married again, but after her second husband died she returned, penniless, to live at Barnsley Gardens with her daughter. Addie had listened to all of her mother's stories about her grandfather and the troubles that had come to the family home. After her mother's death, Addie became determined to restore the mansion, as much as her grandfather had been to build it. In the process she learned of the ghosts of Barnsley Gardens, reflecting its history and the chain of human tragedy.

The ghost Addie knew best, both from stories told to her by neighbors and relatives and by its own admissions, was that of her grandmother Julia. This spirit often materialized near the boxwoods in the garden where Godfrey communed with her after her tragic death. For as long as she lived at Barnsley Gardens, Addie saw her grandmother's mournful spirit in the garden.

On occasion she also saw Robert Earle, the courageous soldier whose body was buried in the garden. He is said to wander the garden near where he was shot and killed, clad in his Confederate gray uniform and wearing a lost, forlorn look. Other ghosts included children whose laughter could be heard in a deserted wing of the house and the ghostly carpenters who hammered and moved heavy objects late at night, intent on completing work on the house.

One ghost that Addie heard more than she saw was that of Godfrey Barnsley. During his life, Godfrey was extremely industrious, rising early and working on his shipping correspondence and plans throughout the day. To reward himself for his industriousness, he had a pre-dinner drink every afternoon around 4:30. Servants and family knew it was time for his drink when they heard the chair at Godfrey's desk scrape along the floor in his study. Addie heard this sound on countless occasions. She concluded that Godfrey's ghost continued to toil in the afterlife since his business often brought him the kind of fulfillment that his personal life lacked.

Addie later married a chemist and took the surname Saylor. Although the couple was passionately committed to restoring Barnsley Gardens, they never had sufficient capital to carry out the costly renovations. But just as things were looking up, tragedy struck once again.

Addie had a son named Preston. Under the name K.O. Dugan (also the name of a character in the film *On the Waterfront*), he became a prizefighter of some repute, and donated much of his earnings to the upkeep of his beloved Barnsley Gardens. Unfortunately, the physical punishment of boxing slowly robbed Preston of his faculties, forcing him to quit the sport. When he became severely unstable, he was committed to a mental asylum near Milledgeville.

During his stay, Preston's mind raced with paranoid delusions. He became convinced that his less adventurous brother, Harry, who now lived at the house, had kept him in confinement and was trying to steal away his share of Barnsley Gardens. (In fact, something like the opposite was true. Harry's return after service in World War I gave Addie new hope for the restoration of the estate.)

After Preston broke free of the asylum in 1935, he made his way to Barnsley Gardens armed with a pistol. He shot Harry in the living room as Addie looked on in disbelief. The former soldier died in his mother's arms, and Preston was sentenced to life in prison.

It was just another tragic episode in the history of Woodlands.

Addie lived at Barnsley Gardens for another seven years. She watched as vines covered the house and the gardens were overtaken by weeds and rot. After her death in 1942, the estate and whatever furnishings remained were sold at auction. Barnsley Gardens was later purchased by W. Earl McClesky and used for farming.

In 1988 a Bavarian prince called Hubertus Fugger bought Barnsley Gardens, sight unseen. He and his wife, Princess Alexandria, have restored the property to its past glory. In a move that would have pleased Godfrey, they planted many exotic and attractive species, such as heirloom rhododendrons, camellias and roses, in the restored gardens. Even more remarkably, the couple also asked two Cherokee chiefs to call off the notorious curse. Today a successful golf resort occupies the land surrounding the house, and visitors are able to explore what remains of the house and learn about the Barnsleys in the Barnsley Family History Museum.

Colonel Fish's House
OGLETHORPE / AMERICUS

As a district court judge, Colonel Fish was a busy, sophisticated man with many friends. He built the house on Randolph Street shortly after he and his wife arrived in Oglethorpe from Pulaski County in 1852. The colonel regularly traveled from Oglethorpe to Macon to conduct his legal affairs. One day, as we shall see, this routine became fatal, and ultimately caused his grumpy ghost to return to his home during a renovation many years later.

Colonel Fish modeled his home on those owned by wealthy British planters in the West Indies. It was altogether unlike the Greek Revival homes fashionable at the time. Two staircases rose diagonally from the ground to the front door on the first-floor portico, giving the impression that the entrance was on the second floor when it was actually the main floor. The basement, whose door and windows were visible from the front, stood above ground. To enhance the foreign feel of the property, Fish ordered trees and flowers from afar and planted them on the grounds. The large windows were the most conspicuous feature. They kept the colonel's reading parlor lit from dawn to dusk, allowing him to indulge in reading, his favorite pastime.

As the colonel's stature grew, high society gatherings became a regular occurrence at the Fish household; guests included prominent attorneys, newspapermen and legislators. More informal gatherings of lawyers and colleagues took place when a particularly interesting or important case was at trial.

Colonel Fish's extensive social network often required him to make weekly trips to Macon and Americus. He would buy a two-way ticket at the station and return later the same night. He did this one morning in 1871. Little did he know that as he walked to the depot, John Holsenbeck and Jim Loyd watched intently from a nearby sidewalk. Spurred on by his friend, and for reasons unknown to this day, Holsenbeck had resolved to kill the colonel.

The pair was convinced that they could get away with the murder. Loyd was an avid gun enthusiast, and when he got wind that one of the colonel's guns was in the local gun shop, waiting to be picked up, Loyd went into the store. He noticed the gun on the shelf and begged the store owner to let him use it to shoot squirrels, promising to return it before its owner would have need of it. The proprietor agreed.

Loyd quickly prepared the proper wadding for the weapon and handed it to his friend. Holsenbeck went to the courthouse alone and withdrew behind a recessed staircase, his sweaty right hand wrapped around Fish's gun. He waited in the darkness until he heard the whistle of the Macon train at the station. As soon as he saw Colonel Fish walk in front of him on his way from the depot to his house, Holsenbeck jumped out of the shadows and shot him. The colonel fell to the ground, dead. Holsenbeck fled the scene, unseen in the darkness, and joined up with Loyd. "Did you get him?" asked his friend. "Yes," he replied. "He's dead."

The body was not discovered until the next morning. Several people had heard the gunshot the night before, but had paid no attention. Mrs. Fish had assumed that her husband had worked late and stayed overnight in Macon with colleagues, as he occasionally would.

The county coroner arrived at the scene and quickly declared the death a homicide. Although Oglethorpe was a major city of 16,000 at the time, once considered for the capital, a small-town attitude gripped the citizens as they gathered to view the dead colonel. Fish was a prominent citizen, so his loss would not go unnoticed. One sentiment dominated all the speculation: his murderer must be found and executed.

Holsenbeck happened to be standing in the crowd. To discourage his connection to the killing, he feigned outrage at the cold-blooded murder and even helped to move the victim's body into a casket. He figured that his well-known reputation for helpfulness would prevent him from coming under suspicion.

The day of the funeral arrived. Many citizens from surrounding towns and counties gathered in the Fish house to pay their last respects. Mrs. Fish, understandably distraught by her husband's death, knelt before his coffin and whispered some telling words: "If the man who committed this heinous deed is here now, let him come forward, touch my husband on the head and confess his crime."

Holsenbeck was once again in attendance. Having become sharply attuned to the most insignificant peep about the murder, he heard her words but remained stone silent, clenching his fists and gritting his teeth. He quickly left the house.

Murder had a strange effect on Holsenbeck's mind—he was racked with guilt. What consumed him was not so much sympathy for the dead man or even his family, but rather the sheer gravity of the deed. Night after night he twisted and turned in bed, reliving an act that took mere seconds but threatened to haunt him forever. He wanted to be free of it.

The people of Oglethorpe, meanwhile—and in many places across Georgia—spoke of little but the investigation. No suspects had been singled out, and the local authorities were at a loss. Hearing this, Rufus B. Bullock, the governor of Georgia and a friend of the dead colonel, sent two detectives named Murphy and Raspberry to find those responsible.

Several days into their investigation, interviews with locals had failed to turn anything up. One day the two detectives walked into a shop where Holsenbeck was. Upon noticing them, he became nervous and uncomfortable. Murphy noticed this behavior, and in a strange but highly effective move, he picked up a woven fish basket and held it up to his face. He peered through the slits in the bottom until his eyes met Holsenbeck's. Then, to test him, he said, "Holsenbeck, you are the guilty man."

Much to the shock of the two detectives, Holsenbeck confessed on the spot. He was quickly arrested, and Loyd was taken into custody shortly thereafter.

Murphy and Raspberry, however, needed more evidence. To collect it, they set up an unorthodox trap. Before the men were placed in their prison cell, the detectives had a large box made to look like a washstand and placed it inside. Then they crawled in and waited for the prisoners to talk to each other, so they could overhear what was said.

The detectives were not disappointed. Assuming they were alone, Holsenbeck and Loyd spoke freely of their crime. Both had been driven to distraction by the pressure of the investigation and the growing public outrage. Loyd, the more level-headed of the two, tried to reassure Holsenbeck, not realizing that they had just unwittingly given all the necessary evidence to the investigators.

In June 1871 Holsenbeck and Loyd were convicted of murder. Members of Loyd's family went to Milledgeville to plead for mercy from the newly elected Governor James Smith. None was forthcoming.

The day of the hangings arrived. Many people traveled by train, even from distant counties, to witness the executions. Water was sold for five cents a glass, and people jostled for a view of the grim proceedings. At high noon, Holsenbeck wandered into the yard, haggard from staying up all night. Before he was hanged, he begged for forgiveness from God and those he had hurt.

Loyd was defiant to the bitter end. While his friend was being dispatched, he slouched on the steps of the gallows and spat tobacco juice on his coffin. He refused to admit his complicity in Colonel Fish's death. When both men were dead, a feeling of relief came over the crowd. Some said that the colonel's ghost was also in attendance, and that the rough justice on display pleased his judge's heart.

Holsenbeck's body was later moved to Columbia County for burial. Loyd, as per request, was buried wearing an undershirt and wrapped in a white sheet. He asked that he be interred north to south since it reflected the odd way in which he led his life.

Mrs. Fish sold the house to M.L. Shealy in 1872. It remained in the Shealy family until 1962, when Mr. and Mrs. Donald Nelson moved in. The new owners, of course, were skeptical when former servants of the Shealys told stories of ghosts traipsing about and arguments between immaterial beings.

The Nelsons had the house moved to Americus in 1969. The move was anything but uneventful. Carpenters had been hired to prepare the new foundation at night, but an unknown force kept interfering with the work. Sand and mortar boxes were unexpectedly upset, and tools mysteriously disappeared. When the house was finally settled on its new plot, a number of small accidents prevented work from being completed on schedule.

In time, and with a great deal of patience, the Nelsons finally restored the house to its original splendor. But just as they were feeling at home, the ghost of Colonel Fish materialized and offered his opinion on the recent relocation.

Mr. Nelson was dozing by the fire when it happened. A lean, dark-haired man in old-fashioned clothing suddenly appeared before him, surprising him out of his half-slumber. In a story in the *Macon Telegraph and News* in 1973, Mr. Nelson said, "I was not really asleep. He told me he was very upset about the house being moved. However, since we were restoring it to his liking, he was happy and peaceful."

The next set of owners, Dr. and Mrs. Gatewood Dudley, sensed the colonel's presence as well. Whenever Dr. Dudley would sit in a certain chair in the front parlor, near where Colonel Fish liked to read so long ago, he reported an otherworldly sensation. Eventually he and his wife took to calling the velvet chair "Colonel Fish's chair," even though it never belonged to him. Dudley suspected that the colonel remained an avid reader in the afterlife, and preferred to have the study to himself.

Culver Kidd Drugstore

MILLEDGEVILLE

Everybody knows that a cataclysmic event can change a person forever. But when a tragic turn of events befalls an inanimate object, it can have a similar effect, changing both the object and the owner forever.

Such was the case with a historic building in Milledgeville, which was damaged in a severe fire that destroyed an adjacent building. Somehow the building's owner could never return to normal following the blaze, and as a reminder of this change, his ghost haunted the building for many years.

At 2 AM on a muggy night in 1926, smoke began to rise from the Elks building at the intersection of Wayne and Hancock streets in downtown Milledgeville. Earlier the same night, a waiter had left an iron on in the basement, and it eventually shorted out and caught fire. Soon flames consumed the entire three-story structure.

As with many commercial fires, adjacent buildings were affected. The one next door, the Culver Kidd Drug Company, had been run by two generations of pharmacists from the Kidd family. Culver Kidd did not follow in his father or grandfather's footsteps, but chose politics as his profession, eventually becoming a state representative and then a senator. The Milledgeville native represented the interests of his friends and neighbors for close to 50 years until his retirement in 1992.

On the fateful night, Culver's father was phoned and notified that the drugstore had caught fire. When the family arrived on the scene, they were relieved to learn that it was the Elks on fire and not their two-story business. Not taking any chances, they began to remove merchandise from their store, aware that the Elks could collapse on their drugstore as the flames consumed it. A woman helping out at the scene was nearly injured when a beam crashed down beside her.

Oddly enough, the person most adversely affected by the fire, J.R. Smith, was not present during the fire. For many years the elderly man had operated a small tailoring business on the second floor of the drugstore. Unlike the drugstore, however, which suffered virtually no damage, the roof of Smith's business and several of the walls were badly charred in the blaze. The Kidds promptly repaired the damage, but Smith never seemed the same: he died, apparently of natural causes, not long after the fire.

Soon after, the Kidds began to hear strange sounds on the second floor of the drugstore—it seemed that the old tailor's spirit had not died with his body. They could hear him shuffling about upstairs for years, and occasionally it sounded as if he was talking to the customers. Whenever the Kidds shifted the furniture around on the second floor, Smith's ghost disapproved. Soon after, they could hear the sounds of furniture moving about; when they inspected, they realized everything was returned to where it had been. For the most part, Smith was a benevolent specter, and the Kidds grew accustomed to the movements.

So why did Smith's ghost remain? Having worked in the store for much of his life, it's likely that he was simply too attached to leave and that he wanted to continue with his work in the afterlife.

Senator Kidd died in December 1995, and reports of Smith's ghost have not occurred since then.

Winecoff Hotel

ATLANTA

During a cataclysmic hotel fire in Atlanta in 1946, a photographer named Arnold Hardy captured an image of a woman (one of many) jumping from the eleventh story of a building. The fire, in which 119 people perished, is still considered the deadliest in U.S. history, and has become the source of some fascinating ghost stories.

At the time, Hardy worked in a research lab at Georgia Tech. Still awake in the early morning hours of December 7, around 3:30 AM he heard a cacophony of sirens blaring several blocks away. He phoned the fire department, identifying himself as a press photographer, and learned that the Winecoff Hotel was on fire. Not hesitating, he grabbed his Speed Graphic camera and summoned a taxi to 176 Peachtree Street.

Soaring to 15 stories, the Winecoff was Atlanta's tallest building when it was finished in 1913. But in a *Titanic*-like stroke of hubris, its builder, William Fleming Winecoff, mistakenly assumed that the building's surrounding layer of brick made it fireproof and even advertised it as such. No fire escapes were installed, and no fire doors were placed around the central staircase. The regulations of the day stipulated that only buildings with a base measuring more than 5000 square feet required sprinklers. The Winecoff fell just shy of this mark, so none were installed.

After a series of fires in the neighborhood in the 1930s, civic authorities imposed stricter fire codes in 1943, requiring the installation of fire safety measures. Unfortunately, these new regulations applied only to new buildings; the city attorney allowed existing structures such as the Winecoff Hotel to remain unchanged. The stage was set for disaster.

It was a cold winter night, and the hotel's 150 rooms were filled to capacity with 280 guests. Some lived there indefinitely, such as Winecoff and his wife, who would both perish in the accident. Most were overnighters—a group of teenagers had come to Atlanta from all over the state for a mock legislature session, and other guests had come to recognize the fifth anniversary of Pearl Harbor in a public ceremony.

Around 3:30 AM, an employee smelled smoke inside the hotel and summoned the fire department. The hotel had a single elevator requiring an operator, and the central stairwell had no doorways on the way down, turning it into an enclosed chimney in the event of a fire.

By the time Hardy arrived and started snapping photos, the fire had already spread throughout the building. Firefighters doused the inferno with water while trying to reach stranded, frantic guests who gasped for fresh air under the thick smoke billowing out of their windows on the upper floors. For those who had crept out onto the window ledges, the building's height was a serious concern. Jumping from any height higher than two stories would mean broken limbs or worse. The ladders on the fire engines were an alternative, but not for everyone: because they stretched to only 85 feet, firefighters could reach evacuees no higher than the eighth floor.

Richard Muns of Augusta was only eight at the time, but he later recalled the ordeal related by his father and uncle, both survivors. The two plumbers were on a business trip and had booked a room in the Winecoff. They awoke too late to escape down the stairs, so they quickly knotted all of their sheets together to make a makeshift rope. Tying it to a radiator, they shimmied down the brick building, moving gingerly for fear that the knots would come apart at any second. Suddenly they heard a scream from above. A little girl had fallen from a window several stories up. She struck Muns' father on her way down, then plummeted to her death on the street below.

To match such tragedies were some remarkable acts of heroism. James D. Cahill, set to enroll in Georgia Tech after a stint in the military, was staying with his mother on the sixth floor in a room at the back of the building. According to Sam Heys and Allen B. Goodwin, authors of *The Winecoff Fire: The Untold Story of America's Deadliest Hotel Fire*, Cahill quickly escaped out the front of the building after the fire broke out, then raced around to the back to rescue his mother. Not seeing an easy way to have her lowered to the ground, he entered an adjacent building and found a strong board, which he laid over a 10-foot alley to the window sill in his mother's room. He then crawled slowly across the board, took his dazed mother on his back and transported her to safety. Impressed with this maneuver, firefighters rushed to Cahill's side and together they rescued many others who were stranded in the back section of the hotel.

Even Hardy pitched in—well, sort of—after he had blown all his flash bulbs and captured all the photographs he needed. Upon overhearing a fireman and a policeman discuss whether to enter a nearby drugstore in search of emergency medical supplies, the intrepid photographer waltzed

The Winecoff Hotel fire is still considered the deadliest in U.S. history.

over and simply kicked the door down. He was arrested on the spot.

Fortunately, he was soon released on his own recognizance and raced to his lab at Georgia Tech to develop his rolls. One of the images, taken at an extremely fast shutter speed, showed a woman as she jumped from a ledge on the eleventh floor, her white skirt billowing from the updraft. It was a brilliant photograph, perfectly capturing the desperation of the moment. Hardy hoped it and the others would draw attention to the lackluster measures in place to deal with a cataclysmic event like the Winecoff fire.

His work done, Hardy ran to the Associated Press office downtown. He was offered $150 for exclusive rights to the photo, but he demanded $300, which he got, plus a $200 bonus the following day. The picture ran in newspapers across the world and won Hardy the Pulitzer Prize a few months later, making him the first ever amateur to earn such an honor. News of the fire, it should be noted, helped to alter fire code regulations across the nation.

For many years, it was thought that the woman in Hardy's award-winning photo perished in the fall. It has since become clear that Daisy McCumber, a secretary who was 41 at the time, survived in spite of breaking both legs, her pelvis and her back. Her extensive injuries required a spate of operations and left her without a leg, but she never admitted to being the woman in Hardy's photo during her life—not even to her family. Like many who survived the fire, she was reluctant to relive the horrific events of December 7, 1946.

The building's subsequent fortunes further wrapped its past in silence. The Winecoff became the Peachtree Hotel in the 1950s and later served as a retirement home. Narrowly escaping demolition in the 1980s, it was successfully auctioned in 1990. Although plans were made to renovate 176 Peachtree Street in the late 1990s, they never materialized, so the building remained vacant.

But history is not easily forgotten. In 1994 one of the fire survivors succeeded in having a State Historic Marker placed at the building. Firefighters, survivors and their relatives attended the ceremony, which saw some tearful, long-overdue reunions.

This emotional closure, mind you, has not erased all the Winecoff's mysteries. The fire, for instance, was initially attributed to a cigarette butt that ignited a bed. But in their book, Sam Heys and Allen B. Goodwin, whose parents survived the blaze, propose that arson was involved, and blame a career criminal who had died in prison. Though their theory is unproveable, it is worth considering, especially in light of the 10 years of research that went into the book.

As for ghost sightings, most of them have been reported by passersby who have seen horrified faces in the upper windows of the vacant building. These have recurred since the 1960s, and tend to happen around 3 AM on chilly winter nights—around the same time that the fire blazed so many years ago.

One of the ghost stories involved Paul Miller, an electrician who was summoned to check the building's power panels in 1985. No stranger to creepy old buildings, Miller was accustomed to squeaks and scratches that would drive anyone else to distraction.

Inside it was dark, with various piles of old building materials lying about. For some unknown reason an old mattress lay in a corner, leading Miller to suspect that squatters had spent some time inside.

Miller got down to work, accomplishing a lot but anticipating at least another full day on site. When he arrived the next morning, he noticed that his tools had been moved. Ordinarily he didn't notice such things, but he remembered very specifically having left them in a certain spot so he could simply pick up where he had left off. He again thought of the squatters, but he realized that they would have stolen the tools since they could easily be sold for a lot of money. So how had they moved? No believer in the paranormal, Miller shook his head and carried on.

Eventually Miller made his way to the basement, where he had to do some rewiring and install a handful of light sockets. As he surveyed the situation, he sighed. To win the contract, he had to put in a very reasonable estimate in terms of time: he figured he could knock off the entire job in a couple days. Now he realized that it would take at least three days, which would put him behind schedule for his next contract. So he decided to work late into the night to finish the job. After eating at a local greasy spoon and filling up on coffee refills, he returned to the old hotel.

Sometime around 1 AM, Miller heard some strange sounds on the floor above, so he went upstairs to make sure that he had locked the doors behind him. He had, so he returned downstairs. As soon as he picked up his tools again, the sounds returned, this time with renewed intensity; it sounded as if people were running around and shouting on the floor above. With his annoyance growing, Miller shouted upstairs, "I'm calling the cops! Now get out of here!" The sounds continued.

He grabbed his flashlight and ran up the old stairwell. When he arrived, the sounds ceased again, but a horrible odor hung in the air, almost like burnt hair. Covering his nose, Miller looked around. "Hello? Is something on fire?" Again, there was no response. As he turned around to survey the situation with his flashlight, the electrician noticed an extra shadow on the wall. He spun around and saw a vision that he remembers to this day.

A woman floated before him in a fluttering dress. It almost seemed as if wind was lifting the skirt from under her—as if she was falling. Her luminescence lit up the entire room, then she disappeared through a wall.

Miller was dumbfounded. He left the site immediately, leaving his tools behind him. When morning came he felt safe to return. He collected his tools and finished his work, but he was unable to get the vision of the woman out of his head. When he contacted the woman who had hired him, she told him about the building's history. Miller became convinced that the woman he saw was a ghost who became trapped in the hotel. Her horrific memories have prevented her from leaving. Needless to say, Miller never took another contract at the old Winecoff Hotel.

7

Crazies and Famous Ghosts

Marion Stembridge
MILLEDGEVILLE

During his freshman year, David Jones lived in a historic boardinghouse on the corner of Georgia and Montgomery streets in Milledgeville. The rather nondescript old property had been converted into a dormitory by Georgia College, where Jones was beginning his studies in geography. Initially the Augusta native was excited about the small room on the second floor, as it was his first place of his own, away from his parents.

On his second night in the room, Jones heard something unusual around 1 AM. It sounded vaguely like jangling keys, so Jones thought it was someone trying to get into the room. He wanted to get up and approach the door, which he had remembered to lock, but something—fear, probably—kept him frozen in bed. The sounds stopped after half an hour or so. By then, Jones had determined the noise was indeed a key jangling in a lock, followed by the "click" of a padlock being opened. Only there was no padlock on his door, nor any in his room. Jones became more bewildered as the night progressed, but he needed sleep, so he just put in his earplugs (a gift from his mom) and eventually nodded off.

The next night there was more of the same, but now the sounds were preceded by heavy footfalls. When he first heard them, Jones bolted up and turned on the light, but as soon as he did, the sounds ceased. Twenty minutes later they were back, so Jones decided to sleep with a lamp on in the room.

For two or three nights this new measure worked, but soon it became difficult for Jones to sleep with the light on all night. Besides, he reasoned, how could he let someone (or something) scare him out of his very own room? While in class one day, he got a brilliant idea: he would buy the loudest window air-conditioner he could find and blast it on HIGH to drown out the sounds. Not only would the annoyance end, but he could also stay cool in an otherwise stuffy room, and the white noise just might lull him to sleep.

Jones bought a big unit the next day and screwed it into the window frame. Yet regardless of how loud he turned the unit, the sounds of steps and keys jangling were always louder. Every night the battle continued. Jones' trusty earplugs blocked out the noise, but they often messed with his ability to sleep peacefully and prevented him from hearing his alarm in the morning.

After three or four weeks, and with midterms approaching, Jones became concerned about all the sleep he was losing. He approached the tenants in the house, asking about the sounds. They responded exactly as he had expected: they had heard nothing. Desperate for answers, Jones decided to ask his neighbors in the house next door, allowing for the possibility that the sounds could originate outside the house. When a building supervisor told Jones about a former resident named Marion Stembridge, one of Milledgeville's most notorious citizens, his curiosity was piqued.

He went to the college's humanities library to learn more. Stembridge's story was fascinating—so much so, in fact, that it had inspired an award-winning novel, *Paris Trout* by Pete Dexter, as well as a movie with the same title starring Dennis Hopper. Was his cruel ghost still haunting the property he once owned?

Jones heard something that sounded vaguely like jangling keys.

It all started with a bad loan in 1949. Stembridge was a successful grocery manager, but his real source of income was a private, unincorporated bank that he ran out of the back of his store. Lending mostly to lower income families and charging outrageous interest, Stembridge accumulated a small fortune over the years—some estimate as much as a million dollars—but also developed very little patience for lateness or excuses.

One day in August, a client of Stembridge's named John Cooper surreptitiously left a sleek black sedan in front of the Stembridge grocery. Cooper assumed that the note he left on the windshield, reading "You can have this pile of steel in exchange for my note," nullified his loan and whatever interest had accrued. Stembridge had different notions. When he found the car and note, he was furious and immediately summoned one of his employees, Sam Terry, to accompany him to Cooper's house to demand payment in full. In the event of a confrontation—a strong possibility, given Stembridge's bitter temper—he wanted someone who could act as a witness.

Stembridge and Terry drove to a rundown area of Milledgeville. Cooper spotted the pair as they arrived and dashed toward a one-room shanty for safe harbor. His assailants caught up with him, hauled him into the street and beat him mercilessly with brass knuckles. Neighbors heard the ruckus and rushed out to peel the two men off their friend. It was then that Stembridge produced a .38 caliber pistol and started firing wildly, hitting two women. One of them, Emma Johnekin, later died.

When police arrived to investigate, they found Stembridge standing defiantly at the scene, with arms crossed and no weapon in sight. He had handed it off to his loyal assistant, who was poised to take the fall. The woman who survived later testified that Stembridge was the only gunman that day.

The next day, the police arrived at Stembridge's residence with a warrant. According to Eugene Ellis, the former chief of police, the loan shark was armed with two guns at the time—a habit, apparently—and when the officers entered his residence, he drew one on them. Stembridge had to be wrestled to the ground and dragged away into custody.

Careful observers could have predicted such a sequence of events. Marion Stembridge was a twisted loner of a man with a history of mental instability; he had been admitted to the Central State Hospital for the Insane on several occasions by his mother. Like many psychopaths, he thrived off a certain sense of impunity—the notion that he could behave as he saw fit, with no regard for others and their feelings, and that no one would catch him. Yet in secret he was extremely paranoid about clients, police, relations—everyone.

Stembridge moved out of his boardinghouse (the one where Jones lived) and rented out the top floor of the Baldwin Hotel in downtown Milledgeville. He kept his large wads of small bills (reflecting his suspicion of the authorities), as well as his beloved guns, in safes hidden throughout the place. He outfitted every cupboard and drawer with heavy locks, even placing a large one on his refrigerator door to prevent his own wife from poisoning him. She left him soon enough, and his descent into paranoia and hatred continued. The first shooting incident and subsequent trial, as it would turn out, were only the opening chapters.

On the stand at his trial, Stembridge claimed self-defense, saying that the women he had shot had been armed. No evidence supported this claim, so he was sentenced to one to three years in prison. Stembridge promptly appealed and was set free on bond until his next trial.

Ballistics tests submitted during the appeal proved that Stembridge was indeed the gunman. A jury deliberated for 13 hours before handing down a unanimous manslaughter charge. But the defendant appealed again, determined to pay no penalty for his crime, and in the end, by writ of *habeas corpus*, it was found that prejudiced testimony had been used against him. He was acquitted, not having served a single day. His accomplice, Sam Terry, also eluded prison on appeals.

Away from the courtroom, Stembridge's banking operation was booming. But while a state-sponsored banking charter and sizeable investments in real estate lent him a veneer of legitimacy, Stembridge himself was becoming more and more twisted—especially in light of his victory in the trial, in which he had gotten away with murder.

Such was the estimation of Marion Ennis, now the District Attorney. Ennis, who had removed himself from the first defense team citing personal apprehensions over Stembridge, now wanted to reopen Stembridge's case and secure a conviction with the help of another attorney, Stephen T. Bivins, who was equally keen on seeing justice served.

Then came a surprise development. The IRS, possibly working off a lead from Bivins, learned that Stembridge had not paid taxes in more than a decade. When agents appeared at his house to read the charges, Stembridge tried to bribe them with $10,000 cash. They were not persuaded, and on April 28, 1953, Stembridge was charged with bribery and ordered to appear for sentencing a week later. Meanwhile, Ennis and Bivins had uncovered evidence of perjury during Stembridge's first trial and set out to reopen the case. The walls were beginning to close in on Marion Stembridge.

On May 3, 1953, citizens of Milledgeville were in the middle of preparations for the 150th anniversary of the city's selection as the Georgia capital. Locals had hung banners, planned a parade and encouraged people from neighboring counties to attend. No one had the slightest inkling that the day would be burned into memory for reasons other than civic pride.

The morning was like any other for Stembridge. Right after lunch he slipped away from his store, telling a clerk he was off to pick up his mother to watch the parade with her; instead, he went to Ennis' office. Ennis, who was alone at the time, was somewhat taken aback by his surprise visitor, and before he could say a thing, Stembridge produced his pistol and shot Ennis repeatedly in the chest and abdomen. The attorney slumped over in his chair, dead, leaving a wife and two small children to mourn him.

Stembridge left the building quietly, headed in the direction of the Standford Building nearby. He calmly climbed the stairs to the second floor where Stephen Bivins kept his office (in what is now the Campus Theater building). He entered, aimed his pistol and shot him twice. Bivins was quicker to react than Ennis and was able to reach frantically into his desk drawer and grab his own gun, hoping to return fire. But he was too weak from the gunshot wound and died before he could pull the trigger.

When the police arrived at Bivins' office, all armed with shotguns, they were afraid that Stembridge was holed up inside, ready to open fire on anyone who approached. When they finally made it inside, they discovered the grocery manager/loan shark dead on the floor. He had chosen suicide over captivity.

So the mystery of David Jones' boarding house spook began to be resolved. Jones took the story of Marion Stembridge to heart, and began to suspect that his ghost was still around and as ornery as ever. The locking noises seemed to reflect Stembridge's paranoia, while his persistence was in keeping with his crusty side and utter lack of respect. Realizing that he could never convince a ghost such as Stembridge to change his stubborn ways, Jones asked the housing board if he could live elsewhere. At first the administration laughed at the freshman's reason—a *ghost* living in the room?—but Jones persisted and eventually got his way. He was happy in his new residence, but he maintained an interest in the goings-on in his old room.

Out of curiosity one day, the freshman returned to his old place in the evening to see if anyone had moved into the haunted room. A friend in the house informed him that it had not yet been filled, probably because the semester was halfway over and it was therefore difficult to find a new tenant.

Jones wandered upstairs and tried the door. It was open. Since it was getting late, he decided to stay awhile to see if his nemesis was still up to his usual tricks. The room was partly furnished, so he sat down at his old desk and began to read a book. Around 11 PM he thought he heard something, but it was only the sound of someone putting garbage in the trash can outside. An hour later, Jones grew impatient and decided to leave. On his way out the door, he saw something in the darkened hallway. "Hello?" he ventured, assuming it was a tenant who lived down the hall. "Jared?"

There was no answer. As Jones squinted for a better look he saw a manifestation of some sort, solidly built and deliberate, move toward the stairs. It moved over the floor, not on it. "Wait!" Jones whispered, trying to keep his voice down. But it was too late. The ghost had disappeared. Jones tried to contact Jared the next day to ask if he had emerged from his room the night before. But Jared's phone message made it clear that he was away and wouldn't be back for a month or two. Jones never returned to the house.

Today, the grocery store Marion Stembridge once ran is now a popular bakery owned by the Ryal family. No ghosts have been reported there to date.

Sam Walker

MILLEDGEVILLE

Small towns have their legendary heroes, and they have their legendary villains, too. In the case of Sam Walker, Milledgeville's least-liked citizen, the stories of his greed and callousness, even involving his own son's death, appear to have grown wildly out of proportion. While the truth about Walker may never emerge, accounts of mysterious happenings in the house where he once lived are undeniable, adding to the mystique surrounding one of Georgia's most infamous characters.

Samuel R. Walker was born on September 4, 1835, in Putnam County, Georgia. Little is known about his early life, but during the Civil War we know he served in the Confederate Army. He began to deal in mortgages and lending notes following the war. Through calculated business dealings, Walker appears to have used estate holdings, some obtained through marriage, to emerge from poverty and become a successful, if excessively shrewd, businessman.

In the late 1860s Walker came to Milledgeville, then the state capital, and bought the house on the corner of Jefferson and McIntosh streets. Among the renovations he made were a mansard room and a Victorian porch. He lived there with his second wife Molley, Molley's niece Alice, whom the couple had recently adopted, and Joel, his only son.

During Reconstruction, times were tough. Georgia had been decimated by the dismantling of its industries and the destructive rampage of Sherman's Union forces. After the war, some speculators took advantage of the situation, accumulating discounted property, issuing loans and fore-closing on those who could not repay. Much resentment gathered around such people, since they appeared to prey on miseries caused by the war. Sam Walker, as local lore would have it, was one such parasite.

One story concerned a merciless loan. A man named Captain Whitaker, who owned a sizable estate near Milledgeville, borrowed $2000 from Walker to buy fertilizer for his cotton. Whitaker planned to sell his crop, then pay back the loan and whatever interest had accrued.

Whitaker's crop was excellent that season. He had the cot-ton milled and ginned, then loaded it into wagons so he could transport it to the city. Whitaker could not recall the exact day of repayment stipulated in the loan, but he knew it was soon. Then, unexpectedly, a terrible storm broke out. Worried that his crop would become wet and worthless, Whitaker stowed his wagons under shelter and delayed his trip into the city until the rain had ceased.

It rained for almost a week. So severe was the storm that the Oconee River rose over its banks, making travel over the bridge between Whitaker's plantation and Milledgeville impossible. He was forced to wait until the water receded.

When it did, Whitaker quickly led his wagons into the city and sold his crop. Then he rushed to pay off Walker. Unfortunately, the cotton farmer arrived one day after the loan was due, so Walker cancelled the loan and foreclosed on the captain's property. His pleas for understanding went unheard, and he lost his plantation.

Is this story true? It's hard to say, although it seems exag-gerated. While Walker's label as a hard-headed business-man may be deserved, and was perhaps attributable to his hardscrabble upbringing, his reputation as a scourge to all Milledgevilleans most certainly is not. In fact, Walker served as the mayor of the city for two separate terms. With his careful head for figures and desire to pull Milledgeville out of economic woe, he made a progressive leader, albeit not one without enemies. Among his accomplishments was the establishment of the Middle Georgia Military and Agricultural College. Walker was an avid rose cultivator as well, and made many renovations to his property to accommodate his hobby.

The issue of Walker's many wives is somewhat more complicated. Walker was married four times, and his first two wives died before he did. Katherine Kirkwood Scott, who owned the Walker house for 75 years after Walker's death, is primarily responsible for the many stories that circulate about the "wickedest man in Georgia." In an article in *Georgia* magazine in 1973, she claimed that workers on his plantation in Eatonton saw Walker kill his first wife.

Unfortunately, this story is false. Walker's first wife, in fact, died in 1862 while he was serving in the military. The cause was erysipelas, a highly contagious disease of the skin marked by high fever. They had been married for eight years. Walker's second wife, Mary ("Molley") Dillard died of meningitis along with the children Joel and Alice, as the account below makes clear. The details of his third marriage, to Sallie Harper, are sketchy at best, although it seems they were wed in the early 1870s and probably divorced soon after because Walker had taken a fourth—and final—wife, Clara Fisher. She lived for many years after Walker died. Most of Walker's marriages brought property into his possession in the form of houses or plantations. A bit of a workaholic,

Walker may have neglected his family or treated them with the same detachment he lent to his business dealings.

This brings us to the most notorious story told about Sam Walker, involving his son Joel, who had been sent to the Mercer University in Macon to prepare him for a bright future. When a meningitis epidemic broke out at the school, forcing it to close, Joel returned to Milledgeville. He soon showed signs of infection. His father, as the story goes, refused to believe the boy was ill; he simply thought he was lazy. He sent Joel to replace an overseer at the Boykin Plantation across the Oconee River. Joel returned the next day looking haggard and claiming to be unfit for work. Once again, Walker showed no sympathy and ordered his son back to the plantation. By this point, Joel's stepmother intervened and summoned a doctor. Walker, a notorious spendthrift, was furious. He refused to let the doctor see the boy, and Joel's health steadily worsened.

One night, Joel struggled up the staircase from his room, begging for medical aid. "Father, I'm dying," he declared, to which his father's explosive response was, "Get back to bed!" Joel, it is said, died after falling down the staircase, hitting his head many times along the way.

Worse, he had spread the infection to Molley and Alice. They too died in a matter of days, and Walker was left alone in his giant home.

In years following the boy's death, Walker is said to have seen Joel's ghost in the staircase where he perished. We know this not merely from Walker's own guilty confessions, but from those of some of his friends, who were shocked during poker games when Walker suddenly became pale with fear and claimed some terrifying presence was in the room. Even on his deathbed, after suffering a serious stroke, Walker shouted deliriously about Joel—begging for forgiveness and some respite from the constant presence of his dead son's spirit.

After Walker's death in 1896, new resident Katherine Kirkwood Scott repeatedly heard thumping on the staircase, almost as if someone was falling. Although she took this as a sign of young Joel's ghost, she never saw his spirit or was able to hear the sound close up. Nevertheless, she remained convinced that it was a dramatization of one of the most painful moments in the house's history, and a reminder of Walker's shocking inhumanity. In fact, wherever Walker is discussed in Scott's memoirs, *The Land of Lost Content*, he comes off as a horrible devil.

The truth of the matter may be more mundane. According to research conducted by James C. Turner, a student at the Georgia College and State University, Scott's perspective may have been colored by a real estate deal in which the Scott family purchased the Jefferson Street house from Walker's widow, Clara. Apparently a small extra property promised to the family never came into the Scott family's possession. It's possible that discontent over this sale, along with lingering resentment against the ambitious businessman, caused Scott to characterize Sam Walker in wildly exaggerated terms. Whatever the case, the ghost sightings seem very real.

Juliette Gordon Low
Girl Scout National Center
SAVANNAH

An elegant Regency townhouse is the place where Girl Scout founder Juliette Gordon Low was born. Known simply as "the Birthplace" to Scouts across the nation, the house transforms into a haven for ghosts late at night. For decades, staff members working alone have noted the sounds of phantom footsteps echoing in the house's main stairway, but they add that these sounds are not scary as much as touching—perhaps a fitting tribute to the Gordon family, one of Savannah's most influential.

James Moore Wayne, then the mayor of Savannah, built the pink stucco house on the corner of Bull and Oglethorpe streets in 1818. The interior was distinguished by Egyptian Revival and classical touches popular in the early 19th century. When Wayne was called to Washington to serve as an associate justice of the U.S. Supreme Court, he sold the house to his niece, Sarah, and her husband, William Washington Gordon I, Juliette's grandparents.

Four generations of Gordons inhabited the home over time, until 1953 when the Girl Scouts bought the house. Three years later it became a museum and Savannah's first National Historic Landmark, largely on the basis of Juliette's accomplishment as the youth group's founder.

Juliette was born on October 31, 1860. She became known as "Daisy" to her family and friends, a name that was later used to describe the most junior Girl Scouts. The precocious

Wayne-Gordon House

young girl, the second of six Gordon children, wrote poetry and sketched from an early age, pastimes she carried with her into adulthood. Pets were another interest of hers, in particular dogs and exotic birds.

But while she grew up in the Gordon house, Juliette did not spend much of her life after childhood there. She attended a private school in Virginia as a teenager and later went to an expensive French school in New York City. She traveled extensively across Europe and the United States following college.

In 1886 Juliette married William Mackay Low, the son of a prosperous British shipping magnate, and the two spent most of their time in England and Scotland. A bizarre incident at the wedding came to symbolize Juliette's ability to overcome obstacles. While rice was being tossed at the newlyweds, a grain lodged itself in her ear and became infected. One of the doctors who tried to extract the grain actually pushed it in farther, rupturing her eardrum and causing life-long deafness in her left ear. Like most of the setbacks in her life, Juliette took it as an opportunity to rebound.

Unfortunately, she had to go much of the way alone. William Low was a dour man and a playboy of sorts among the English nobility, and he and Juliette spent many years apart. Juliette was an idealist, much like her passionate mother Nellie. She even assisted Nellie as she offered relief to soldiers during the Spanish-American War. When Juliette returned to England, her marriage was all but over and the couple separated before William passed away in 1905. For several years Juliet searched for inspiration to fill her days.

In 1911 a meeting with Lord Robert Baden-Powell changed her life forever. He explained to her that many girls had tried to join the fledgling organization he had founded, the Boy Scouts. Baden-Powell's sister, Agnes, founded the Girl Guides in England, and when Juliette returned to Savannah as a 52-year-old widow, she used some of Agnes' ideas to organize the first meeting for a troop of 18 "American Girl Guides" (subsequently called Girl Scouts). They took nature walks, cooked meals and earned badges for excellence in different "scouting" activities. Membership expanded quickly, as did the Girl Scouts' role in society at large: they assisted the Red Cross during World War I by offering relief to nurses and selling Liberty Bonds. With more than 2.5 million members today and more than 50 million members in its illustrious history, the Scouts remain the largest girls' group in the world.

Juliette's vision for the Scouts was not merely to provide girls with the skills necessary for domestic life, although this was a key goal, but also to make them self-reliant and resourceful—qualities that would prove invaluable in whichever field they chose later in life. Better still, the Scouts accepted girls regardless of race, creed or religion. Being part deaf, Gordon was eager to welcome girls with disabilities as equals, then a revolutionary notion. For a woman who never had any children of her own, Juliette made an extraordinary impact on the lives of girls everywhere.

Juliette Gordon Low died of breast cancer in 1927. Her posthumous honors included a stamp dedicated by President Harry Truman, a World War II–era ship named for her, inclusion in the National Women's Hall of Fame and a Federal building in her name in Savannah. Today, the Juliette Gordon Low Girl Scout National Center looks as it appeared during Juliette's childhood in the 1860s, except for some important Scout-related memorabilia. As well, a set of iron gates she designed and built for a blacksmithing course still stand outside the garden in the rear of the house.

It is ironic that the Gordon family's most fascinating members were not Juliette and her grumpy husband, who did not live in the family house long. Rather they were Juliette's parents, William Gordon II and Nellie Kinzie, better known as Willie and Nellie, who moved into the home after they married in 1858.

The couple was far from an ideal match. Nellie, whose ancestors came from New England, was a sophisticated woman with a Yale pedigree and an open mind. Willie, on the other hand, was a dyed-in-the-wool Southerner, a defender of slavery and a Presbyterian. Their clashing backgrounds became pronounced during the Civil War, when Willie fought with the Georgia Hussars. Three of Nellie's brothers, meanwhile, fought for the Union side; two were captured while another was killed in combat. Unlike other families divided by the war, however, the Gordons were committed to each other despite differing ideologies.

Nellie grew impatient waiting in Savannah for her husband's return. Using her pull, she had both General Robert E. Lee and General William T. Sherman help her locate him. Eventually, escorted by two Confederate soldiers, she traveled to Virginia and caught up with Willie.

Nellie was not troubled when Sherman's troops overtook the city after she had returned to Savannah. She had hid all the family valuables and was treated with the utmost respect by General Sherman, who put a guard outside her home and allowed her to contact Willie on her way north (all wives of Confederate officers were expected to leave the city).

The family reunited in 1865 in Savannah and reclaimed the Gordon residence. Willie earned additional accolades both as a soldier and a businessman, achieving the rank of brigadier general in the Spanish-American War and acting as the president of the Savannah Cotton Exchange. Flags flew at half mast when he died in 1912, and Nellie's life quickly seemed very empty without him. She had her children and her passions, but Willie was the great love of her life. During her final illness she was reported as saying, "When I die, I don't want…any tears. I shall be so happy with my Willie again that everyone should celebrate." She died in February 1917. According to Mary Stewart Gordon Platt, one of Willie and Nellie's six children, Willie appeared in the house on the day Nellie died. Both Mary and the family butler saw him walk down the stairs, clad in his familiar gray suit, only minutes before Nellie passed away.

The ghost of Nellie has also been identified at the museum. One Sunday evening, as a docent member was preparing to leave, she realized she'd forgotten a book. After asking the woman with the keys to wait for her she rushed up the stairs, not bothering to turn on the light. Then she heard someone moving around in the center hall and took a peek. It was a woman in a white dress, who seemed glad that everyone had finally gone. Although she looked very familiar, the docent was too terrified to figure out who it was, so she dashed down the stairs without having retrieved her book. When she reached the front door, she realized that the spirit was Nellie Gordon, whom she recognized from a portrait in the house. She ran upstairs again, but by then the spirit was gone.

Other mysterious phenomena recur. Long-lost objects suddenly reappear, then move around at night seemingly at random. Once, two of Juliette's paintings were moved from one room to another. The museum director naturally assumed that one of the staff members had notions about interior decorating and asked everyone who was behind the stunt, but no one came forward. Finally, she decided to investigate and had the switched pictures removed from the

She ran upstairs again, but by then the spirit of Nellie Gordon was gone.

wall. They were firmly fastened, so it was difficult for the carpenters to pry them loose. When they did, it seemed as if no new screws had been used, and no new holes appeared in the wall.

When the director consulted the original plans for the museum, she learned that all of Juliette's paintings were to be firmly fastened to the wall, so as never to be moved again. But if this was the case, why did it seem like the switched pictures had never been moved at all? They were obviously out of place, so the walls would inevitably have suffered some damage. But the two paintings in question had been moved seamlessly, almost perfectly. The switch remains a mystery today, but it's possible that the ghost of Nellie or Juliette was simply performing some otherworldly interior decorating.

In a final ghostly encounter, one of the custodians heard pianoforte music echoing through the house after the museum was closed. Naturally he assumed it was a staffer or a straggler who stayed on after closing, and he hoped whoever it was would soon leave. But the music continued to echo very faintly yet distinctly, so the custodian got up to see what was amiss. As he approached the north parlor, where the instrument was kept, he noticed even more clearly how perfectly the music was being played. He found no one in front of the instrument when he arrived, and the music had suddenly stopped. Odder still, the protective cover over the keys appeared to be locked. The next day he asked one of the tour leaders about the instrument. She explained that only a small percentage of the keys actually worked, and that the instrument hadn't been used since Nellie played it back in the beginning of the 20th century.

The Wren's Nest

ATLANTA

This country retreat, the oldest house museum in Atlanta, was once the home of Joel Chandler Harris, author of the beloved "Uncle Remus" tales. But despite all the joy and laughter Harris brought to both his readers and his family, the Harris house includes one tragic memento that cannot be seen during a typical visit: the ghost of his son Linton.

Few could have predicted Harris' rise. He was born on December 9, 1848, in Eatonton. His mother's family disapproved of his father, who disappeared soon after Joel's birth. From his earliest days, Harris loved reading and telling stories. Although he disliked reading in school, he consumed every book he could get his hands on. Encouraged by his mother, who worked as a seamstress and used to read Thomas Hardy's *Vicar of Wakefield* aloud to him, Harris began to write stories of his own at an early age.

The precocious Harris was no mere bookworm, however. He loved to play in the woods, steal peaches from local orchards and ride horses, but his fledgling imagination received the greatest jolt from visits he made to the cabin of George Terrell, a friendly slave and the local patriarch. While they sat in front of a musty old fireplace, "Uncle George," as he was known, spun charming vernacular tales about colorful personalities and history. Harris was entranced, so much so that he later modeled his own creation, Uncle Remus, on the friendly old storyteller.

At 13, Harris became a printer's assistant at *The Countryman*, a newspaper published on a plantation. The Civil War put an

Joel Chandler Harris

end to the paper, so Harris searched elsewhere for work, eventually landing reporting posts on the *Macon Telegraph*, the *New Orleans Crescent Monthly* and the *Savannah Morning News*. He settled in Atlanta, where he wrote a column of "pithy and philosophical sayings" in the *Atlanta Constitution* and later became the paper's co-editor.

One fateful day in 1877, with a deadline for his column looming, Harris was hopelessly blocked: nothing would come out. In a fit of inspiration, with the slave dialect still vivid in his ear, he scribbled down his first Uncle Remus tale and submitted it. The *Constitution*'s readers adored the story, and soon people across the country were interested in reading more.

Harris' column developed into *Uncle Remus: His Songs and Sayings* (1881), which remains a treasury of American folklore. His characters—Brer Rabbit, Brer Bear and Brer Fox—were animals, but showed very human characteristics, much like A.A. Milne's *Winnie the Pooh* characters. Though later called "Georgia's Aesop," Harris downplayed his role in the storytelling, claiming he was "only the compiler" of yarns related by others—yarns with cleverly disguised morals under layers of Southern humor.

During his stint in Savannah, Harris met a charming French-Canadian belle called Esther du Pont LaRose and fell deeply in love with her. The painfully shy Harris at first wooed her in poetic letters, but eventually summoned the courage to ask for her hand in marriage. She accepted, and the couple set out to start a family.

In 1881 Harris rented the house at 1050 Gordon Street, in Atlanta's West End. The country house had been built in 1870 by George Muse, founder of the celebrated George Muse Clothing Company. When the Harrises first arrived, they found the property in a shambles, overrun with weeds, rats and bats. They fixed it up a little and later bought it from the *Constitution*, which had purchased the house in 1883.

Harris hired an architect, George P. Humphreys, to add a large addition to the one-and-a-half-story house. The resulting asymmetrical facade, a model of the Queen Anne style then popular in the Northeast, had a steep, gabled roof and a heavily latticed wraparound porch, where Harris would sit in an old rocker and do most of his writing. An avid gardener, he spent many hours tending to his roses and vegetables and later named the property "Snap Bean Farm."

Harris and his wife had six children. Harris was unusually interested in his children's upbringing—then almost exclusively the province of women. Along with playing with them in the garden, he enjoyed telling the stories he knew almost as much as they enjoyed hearing them. As the children left home, he wanted them to be nearby whenever they could, so he had two small houses erected on the grounds; today, they are private residences. One of Harris' sons, Julian, went on to become the first Georgia recipient of the Pulitzer Prize in 1926 for a series of editorials exposing the Ku Klux Klan.

The family house earned its nickname, the Wren's Nest, when one of the children noticed that a wren had built a nest in the mailbox. Another mailbox was erected to accommodate the birds, and the name stuck.

Over 25 years, Harris compiled nine volumes of Uncle Remus tales from a variety of sources; they have been translated into 27 languages and have influenced a variety of writers, including Rudyard Kipling and Beatrix Potter. The most familiar Uncle Remus tale, "The Wonderful Tar Baby," was dramatized in the 1946 Disney film *The Song of the South.* The film's catchy tune "Zip-a-dee Doo Dah" took the Oscar for Best Song the same year, although its toned-down, "Hollywood" portrayal of Reconstruction race relations has been considered highly controversial, and Disney has withheld the film from video and other television licensing. While Uncle Remus remains the source of his considerable fame, Harris wrote other books, including a history of Georgia and a biography of his co-editor at the *Constitution,* Henry Grady. Taking advantage of his position as a powerful newspaper editor, he was also active in social causes, rallying for increased education for black children and greater

The Wren's Nest

understanding between the North and South to stimulate investment in Atlanta from Northern business interests. Harris was a friend of many celebrated authors, including Mark Twain and James Whitcomb Riley, and he met with President Theodore Roosevelt when he came to Atlanta and later visited him and the First Lady at the White House.

After a long and productive life, Joel Chandler Harris died in 1908. His widow sold the Wren's Nest to the Uncle Remus

Memorial Society in 1913, and it has been open to the public ever since. Apart from first editions of all the Uncle Remus books, as well as signed books by many well-known Southern writers, the memorabilia on display include a diorama of the house donated by Walt Disney and many photographs of the Harris family. The house was designated a National Historic Landmark in 1962.

Harris' seemingly charmed life was not entirely without misfortune. Three of his children died very young. In September 1890, one of them, Linton, fell ill with a sore throat. It seemed like a routine infection until his heart was affected and the seven-year-old died. His family, and in particular his father, was crushed.

Over the years, many sightings of Linton's ghost have been made in the front hall of the house. The boy is clad in old-fashioned children's clothes and wears a look of tender resignation. It's up to visitors to decide what ails him more: his untimely death or not being able to hear his father's stories in the world beyond.

The End